42,49

5

D0340549

embryo

. . . .

Also by Robert P. George
In Defense of Natural Law

Also by Christopher Tollefsen
Biomedical Research and Beyond

Doubleday

New York   London   Toronto   Sydney   Auckland

embryo

. . . . . .

A DEFENSE OF HUMAN LIFE

Robert P. George
and
Christopher Tollefsen

PUBLISHED BY DOUBLEDAY

Copyright © 2008 by Robert P. George and Christopher Tollefsen

All Rights Reserved

Published in the United States by Doubleday, an imprint of The Doubleday
Broadway Publishing Group, a division of Random House, Inc., New York.
www.doubleday.com

DOUBLEDAY and the portrayal of an anchor with a dolphin are registered
trademarks of Random House, Inc.

Book design by Maria Carella

Library of Congress Cataloging-in-Publication Data
George, Robert P.
Embryo : a defense of human life / Robert P. George and Christopher
Tollefsen. — 1st ed.
p. cm.
Includes bibliographical references and index.
1. Embryonic stem cells—Moral and ethical aspects. 2. Human embryo—
Research—Moral and ethical aspects. I. Tollefsen, Christopher. II. Title.
QH588.S83G46 2008
174.2—dc22   2007017585

ISBN 978-0-385-52282-3

PRINTED IN THE UNITED STATES OF AMERICA

1   3   5   7   9   10   8   6   4   2

First Edition

For John Finnis

Contents

Contents

Acknowledgments

The authors have benefited from the assistance, advice, criticism, and support of many people. They wish particularly to thank the Witherspoon Institute, Ryan Anderson, Patrick Lee, Ph.D., Luis Tellez, Carlos Cavalle, Herbert W. Vaughan, Esq., Roger and Carol Naill, Howard and Roberta Ahmanson of Fieldstead and Co., Joe and Debbie Duffy, William Saunders, Esq., Edward Smith, Esq., Ward Kischer, Ph.D., William Hurlbut, MD, Maureen Condic, Ph.D., Richard Doerflinger, Markus Grompe, MD, Thomas Berg, LC, Ph.D., Alfonso Gomez-Lobo, Ph.D., Gilbert Meilaender, Ph.D., Mary Ann Glendon, LL.M., Leon Kass, MD, Ph.D., Edward Furton, Ph.D., Eric Cohen, Yuval Levin, John Finnis, D.Phil., Germain Grisez, Ph.D., Christian Brugger, D.Phil., Hadley Arkes, Ph.D., Daniel N. Robinson, Ph.D., Kevin Flannery, SJ, D.Phil., Nicanor Austriaco, OP, Ph.D., Jane Hale, Bradford Wilson, Ph.D., Laurie Tollefsen, Ph.D., Susan Carstensen.

embryo

.   .   .   .

CHAPTER 1

What Is at Stake
in the Embryo Experimentation
Debate

.   .   .   .   .   .

NOAH AND THE FLOOD

On January 16, 2007, a remarkable journey came to an end in Covington, Louisiana. Sixteen months earlier, Noah Benton Markham's life had been jeopardized by the winds and rain of Hurricane Katrina. Trapped in a flooded hospital in New Orleans, Noah depended upon the timely work of seven Illinois Conservation Police officers, and three Louisiana State officers who used flat-bottomed boats to rescue Noah and take him to safety.

Although many New Orleans residents tragically lost their lives in Katrina and its aftermath, Noah's story of rescue is, nevertheless, one of many inspirational tales of heroism from that national disaster. What, then, makes it unique? And why did the story of his rescue end sixteen months *after* the events of September 2006? The answer is that Noah has the distinction of being one of the *youngest* residents of New Orleans to be saved from Katrina: when the Illinois and Louisiana police officers entered the hospital where Noah was trapped, he was an embryo, a human being in the very earliest stages of development, frozen with fourteen hundred embryos in canisters of liquid nitrogen.

Noah's story had a happy ending: Noah's parents were overjoyed those sixteen months later when Noah emerged, via cesarean section, into the light of the wide world. His parents named him in acknowledgment of a resourceful survivor of an earlier flood. His grandmother immediately started phoning relatives with the news: "It's a boy!" But if those officers had never made it to Noah's hospital, or if they had abandoned those canisters of liquid nitrogen, there can be little doubt that the toll of Katrina would have been fourteen hundred human beings higher than it already was, and Noah, sadly, would have perished before having the opportunity to meet his loving family.

Let us repeat it: *Noah* would have perished. For it was Noah who was frozen in one of those canisters; Noah who was brought from New Orleans by boat; Noah who was subsequently implanted into his mother's womb; and Noah who was born on January 16, 2007.

Noah started this remarkable journey as an embryo, or blastocyst—a name for a very early stage of development in a human being's life. Noah continued that journey after implantation into his mother's womb, growing into a fetus and finally an infant. And he will continue, we are confident, to grow into an adolescent and a teenager as he continues along the path to adulthood.

Noah's progress in these respects is little different from that of any other member of the human race, save for the exertions necessary to save him at the very earliest stage of his life. But in later years, if Noah were to look back to that troubled time in

New Orleans and ask himself whether *he* was rescued that day, whether it was *his life* that was saved, we believe that there is only one answer he could reasonably give himself: "Of course!"

THE MORAL

This answer to Noah's question is a mere two words long, yet it contains the key to one of the most morally and politically troubled issues of our day. Is it morally permissible to produce and experiment upon human embryos? Is it morally permissible to destroy human embryos to obtain stem cells for therapeutic purposes? Is it morally permissible to treat human embryos as disposable research material that may be used and destroyed to benefit others? All such questions have the seeds of their answer in these two words. For what Noah would be saying in these two words—and his answer is confirmed by all the best science—is that *human embryos are, from the very beginning, human beings, sharing an identity with, though younger than, the older human beings they will grow up to become.*

Human embryos are not, that is to say, some other type of animal organism, like a dog or cat. Neither are they a part of an organism, like a heart, a kidney, or a skin cell. Nor again are they a disorganized aggregate, a mere clump of cells awaiting some magical transformation. Rather, a human embryo is a whole living member of the species Homo sapiens in the earliest stage of his or her natural development. Unless severely damaged, or denied or deprived of a suitable environment, a human being in the embryonic stage will, by directing its own integral organic functioning, develop himself or herself to the next more mature developmental stage, i.e., the fetal stage. The embryonic, fetal, child, and adolescent stages are stages in the development of a determinate and enduring entity—a human being—who comes into existence as a single-celled organism (the zygote) and develops, if all goes well, into adulthood many years later.

But does this mean that the human embryo is a human person worthy of full moral respect? Must the early embryo never be used as a mere means for the benefit of others simply because it is a human being? The answer that this book proposes and defends with philosophical arguments through the course of the next several chapters is "Yes."

This "yes" has many implications, for human life in its earliest stages and most dependent conditions is under threat today as in no other era. The United States, as well as many of the countries of Europe and the developed countries of Asia, are about to move beyond the past thirty years' experience of largely unrestricted abortion to a whole new regime of human embryo mass production and experimentation. This new regime requires new rationalizations. Whereas, in the past, the humanity of the fetus, or its moral worth, were ignored or denied in favor of an alleged "right to privacy," or considerations of the personal tragedies of women experiencing unwanted pregnancies, what is now proposed is something quite different.

The production of human embryos, and their destruction in biomedical research, will take place in public labs by teams of scientists. If those scientists and their many supporters have their way, their work will be funded, as it is or soon will be in California, New Jersey, and elsewhere, by the state or by the nation, and in either case by taxpayers' money. And if that work bears fruit, then the consequences of this research will be felt throughout the world of medicine and the pharmaceutical industry.[1] It will be virtually impossible for those with grave moral objections to such experimentation to remain free from entanglement in it: their money will pay for labs in their universities, and their doctors will routinely use the results of embryo-destructive research.

For example, in 2004, a ballot initiative known as Proposition 71 was passed in California. This referendum was supported by Arnold Schwarzenegger, the Republican governor of the state. Its backers contributed a tremendous amount of money, and much propaganda, to ensure its passage. The measure promises that up to $3.1 billion will be spent on embryo-destructive research over the next ten years. Even supporters of the research have pointed out that Proposition 71 threatens to bring about a largely unregulated industry that will inevitably line the pockets of a relative few.[2] But such objections, important as they are, ignore what this industry is centrally about: the production and destruction of human beings in the earliest stage of development. This basic truth is lost amidst discussion of "therapeutic cloning" or "Somatic Cell Nuclear Transfer (SCNT)," euphemisms and technicalities designed to obscure rather than clarify. And amidst the promises of boundless health benefits from this research, it can become tempting to lose sight of all that is really at stake. But consider the following analogy.

Suppose that a movement arose to obtain transplantable organs by killing mentally retarded infants. Would the controversy that would inevitably erupt over this be best characterized as a debate about organ transplantation? Would anyone accept as a legitimate description the phrase *therapeutic organ harvesting*? Surely not: the dispute would best be characterized—and in any decent society it would be characterized—as a debate about the ethics of killing retarded children in order to obtain their organs. (Indeed, in a truly decent society, the question would not arise at all!)

Nor would the public, we submit, accept arguments for the practice that turned on considerations about how many gravely ill nonretarded people could be saved by extracting a heart, two kidneys, a liver, etc., from each retarded child. For the threshold question would be whether it is unjust to relegate a certain class of human beings—the retarded—to the status of objects that can be killed and dissected to benefit others. Similarly, there would be something almost obscene in worrying about underregulation of these procedures.

By the same token, we should not be speaking, as in California, in terms of a debate about embryonic stem cell research; nor is the main moral issue that of adequate governmental oversight. No one would object to the use of embryonic stem cells in biomedical research or therapy if they could be derived without killing or in any way wronging the embryos. Nor would anyone object to using such cells if they could be obtained using embryos lost in spontaneous abortions. The point of the controversy is the ethics of deliberately destroying human embryos for the purpose of producing stem cells. The threshold question is whether it is unjust to kill members of a certain class of human beings—those in the embryonic stage of development—to benefit others. Thus we return to the significance of the story of Noah and the flood.

THE EMBRYO TECHNOLOGIES
OF TODAY AND TOMORROW

What is it, though, that is currently being done with embryos, or that can currently be done with embryos, or that might one day be done with embryos? In this section we describe various embryo technologies, some of which are currently possible, and some that might be on the horizon. Before doing this, however, it is important to make some distinctions. In particular, we need to distinguish between what we will call *embryo science, embryo technology,* and *embryo ethics.*

We distinguish between embryo technology, and technologies, on the one hand, and embryo science, on the other, for a simple reason: Embryo science tells us two important things about human embryos: what they are, and when they begin. It tells us, that is, that human embryos are human beings at a certain (very early) developmental stage, and that in the vast majority of cases, those human beings begin at conception, the initiation of a new single-celled human organism after the fertilization of an egg by a sperm. Science tells us these two things so definitively, in fact, that a whole chapter of this book is devoted simply to the science of embryos. But science itself does not provide us with guidance in making moral decisions about the treatment of those embryos or of human beings at any developmental stage.

Embryo technologies represent the abilities of researchers to do things to or with embryos. And researchers can do many such things. They can make embryos in a lab, whether by in vitro fertilization or by cloning. They can keep embryos alive in the lab, whether in a petri dish, or indefinitely by cryopreservation (freezing). Researchers can then manipulate those embryos by tinkering with their DNA or by introducing foreign DNA, such as animal DNA, into a human embryo's genetic makeup. And, ultimately, researchers can destroy those embryos, extracting cells for the purpose of providing pluripotent stem cell lines.

Like embryo science, embryo technology is incapable of providing moral guidance regarding the question of how we ought to treat those embryos. We know from science that those embryos are nascent human beings; and we know from technological research that we can manipulate those embryos in a variety of destructive ways. But is such manipulation morally right? Is it just? It is the business of moral philosophy—embryo ethics, as we call it here—to answer this question.

It is critical to engage seriously with embryo ethics today. For it is not uncommon to hear embryo researchers and their supporters claim that only science should have a say in what science does, and that ethics, religion, and politics have no business in the concerns of science. Such sentiments should sound familiar to anyone who has listened to proponents of such research defend the freedoms and even the imperatives of scientific research.

Such claims are true in one way and false in another, however. It is true that moral philosophy cannot say what the embryo *is*. Nor does moral philosophy have anything to say about what *can* be done with an embryo. These are matters of the way the world is, and moral philosophy is concerned with what we *ought* to do, or refrain from doing. But by the same token, science, which is concerned with what is the case, has nothing to say about what we ought to do, even in the domain of science.

Moreover, it is clearly false to say that if something can be done, then it ought to be done, or that it would be good to do it.

This was made abundantly clear earlier in our hypothetical story about transplanting the organs of retarded children. It is, sadly, made even clearer by the historical record of the twentieth century. Nazi experiments on handicapped persons, Jews, and others regarded as "undesirables"; the Tuskegee experiments on poor black men; radiation experiments on the unsuspecting carried out by the U.S. military—all testify to the necessity of science accompanied by moral reflection, not the imperative of science unbounded by morality.[3] And, as the following brief look at what is and might soon be the case in embryo technology reveals, now is the time for that reflection.

Some say that the age of embryo technology began on July 25, 1978, with the birth of Louise Brown, the world's first "test tube baby," in England. More accurately, the age of embryo technology began nine months earlier, when Louise herself came into existence in a petri dish under the guidance of doctors Patrick Steptoe and Robert Edwards.[4] Since then in vitro fertilization (IVF) has become a significant way of addressing infertility, with nearly 1 percent of all live births in the United States originating in vitro.

Current IVF techniques are easily understood. In natural human reproduction, a sperm cell from the male penetrates and fertilizes a waiting egg that has been released from the ovary of the mother. (In chapter two, we will give a more detailed account of what happens in this process.) The result of successful fertilization is a new single-celled human organism, the zygote.

In most cases, of course, the means by which the sperm is introduced into the environment of the egg is sexual intercourse between a man and a woman. But in IVF, the meeting of sperm and egg takes place "in vitro," that is, in a petri dish in a lab (although "in vitro" means "in glass," a petri dish is actually made of plastic). Typically, the mother-to-be is given drugs to stimulate ovulation. An ultrasound-guided needle is inserted into one of her ovaries and used to retrieve the eggs. Sperm is obtained from the father, and either many sperm are injected into a solution surrounding an egg, or a single sperm is directly inserted into an egg. When the sperm penetrates the egg, the resulting fertilization process takes place just as it would within the mother. After three days, or a bit more, the resulting embryo or embryos are transferred to the mother's uterus. The mother may receive a hormonal treatment to ensure that her uterine lining remains suitable for implantation.[5]

In a typical IVF procedure, especially in the United States, more eggs are fertilized than are inserted into the mother. In consequence, and sometimes with a view to future pregnancies, extra or surplus embryos are frozen in liquid nitrogen (a process called cryopreservation), where they can remain in a state of suspended animation for a considerable period of time. The existence of these "spare" or "surplus" embryos is bound up with the origins of the controversy over embryo experimentation.

That controversy, in the United States, dates back to 1978 and the early days of IVF. Following Louise Brown's birth, an Ethics Advisory Board (EAB) appointed by Joseph Califano, the secretary of health, education, and welfare, "concluded that research on very early embryos within the first fifteen days of development was acceptable to develop techniques for in vitro fertilization."[6] The Carter administration then allowed the EAB's tenure to expire. Since the National Commission for the Protection of Human Subjects had stated that no experimentation could be performed on IVF embryos unless approved by an

EAB, this effectively blocked embryo research.[7] Neither the Reagan nor the first Bush administrations proposed to reestablish such a board.

The issue of embryo research, and the question of how to obtain embryos for research, was again taken up by two different advisory panels under the Clinton administration. In 1994, the Human Embryo Research Panel (HERP), appointed by the head of the NIH, Harold Varmus, recommended that embryo research be permitted for the purposes of developing IVF techniques and for the study of embryonic stem (ES) cells. Such research was to be performed on "spare" embryos from IVF, provided that informed consent from the parents was obtained. The panel recommended further review for the creation of embryos for the derivation of embryonic stem cells (ESC), but it did argue for federal funding of the creation of embryos for some research purposes. Shortly thereafter, however, President Clinton announced that he was prohibiting the use of federal funds for the creation of embryos.[8]

Congress also responded to the NIH's proposal by appending a rider to the Labor, Health, and Human Services appropriation bill. The Dickey Amendment bans the use of federal funds for any research in which human embryos are harmed or destroyed or created for research purposes.[9]

In 1998, another committee, the National Bioethics Advisory Commission (NBAC), again recommended that destructive research be permitted on human embryos left over from IVF. In opposition to the 1994 HERP recommendations, however, the NBAC "Recommendation Three" reads, "Federal agencies should not fund research involving the derivation or use of ES (embryonic stem) cells from embryos made solely for research purposes using IVF."[10] The commission also recommended against the creation of embryos for research through cloning techniques in "Recommendation Four": "Federal agencies should not fund research involving the derivation or use of human ES cells from embryos made using SCNT into oocytes."[11]

By the time of the NBAC's recommendations, however, two developments in the world of embryo technology had radically changed the technological, moral, and political landscapes. These developments, which have since played a critical role in all debates about the human embryo, were the first mammalian cloning, of a sheep, by Dr. Ian Wilmut, and the first successful isolation of human embryonic stem cells by Dr. James Thomson.

We have referred to "embryonic stem cells" several times already in this book. And every reader has doubtless heard of their remarkable qualities. But what are embryonic stem cells, and why are they considered so important in biomedical research? To answer this question, we need some initial understanding of the nature of the human embryo.

We have suggested, and will argue further, that the early human embryo is a complete, albeit developmentally immature, human being. Yet it is evident to anyone that the differences between the human embryo and the adult human being are tremendous. The adult human being, although composed of cells genetically identical to the early cell or cells that composed him as an embryo, nevertheless has cells that are best described in terms of their particular functions: blood cells, brain cells, heart cells, liver cells, and so on. Yet the young embryo, in its first days, is composed of cells that are not yet differentiated in terms of the functional role they will play in the organism's later life. Rather, it is composed, in its first few days of life, of cells that are capable of developing into any type of cell in the body. Indeed, evidence suggests that if detached from the rest of the embryo of which they are a part, some or all of these cells can develop as a complete human organism, maturing in the same fashion as any human zygote. This quality is referred to as *totipotency*.

A few days after fertilization, as cell division proceeds, the embryo takes the shape of a fluid-filled ball called a blastocyst, which is formed of an inner cell mass and an outer layer of cells. The outer layer generates the cell lineage that will become the placenta (an intrauterine organ of the developing embryo); the inner cell mass is the origin of the lineage that becomes the cells, tissues, and organs of the adult human body. Cells extracted from the inner cell mass can be grown in a laboratory culture and appear to retain this *pluripotency*—i.e., the capacity to form any of the various kinds of tissue in the mature human being.[12]

As the name suggests, a stem cell is a source for other cells. A blood stem cell, for example, can divide into two cells: one a blood cell, the other another stem cell, from which further blood cells can be produced. Maureen Condic, a noted professor of neurobiology and anatomy, summarizes:

> The term "stem cell" is a general one for any cell that has the ability to divide, generating two progeny (or "daughter cells"), one of which is destined to become something new and one of which replaces the original stem cell. . . . There are many stem cell populations in the body at different stages of development. For example, all of the cells of the brain arise from a neural stem cell population in which each cell produces one brain cell and another copy of itself every time it divides. The very earliest stem

cells . . . are termed embryonic stem cells, to distinguish
them from populations that arise later and can be found in
specific tissues.[13]

Embryonic stem cells, then, have not just the potential to
become blood, or neuronal, or liver cells, but the potential to become cells of any type.

It does not take much imagination to see possible uses for
such cells. For if one could obtain them, and direct them in the
right way, then it might be possible to produce blood cells, or
neuronal cells, or liver cells, and perhaps even, in time, complete
organs, for transplant into sick patients. In a 1998 paper, James
Thomson announced that he had taken one step along this path,
producing stem cells from cells taken from the inner cell mass of
a human blastocyst.[14]

There is, however, a cost: the death of the embryonic human
being. But even apart from this obvious moral consideration,
there are many difficulties involved in the project of directing
embryonic stem cells toward particular differentiating functions.
For example, it is unknown what "structural or mechanical elements uniquely associated with the complex environment of the
embryo" are co-responsible for the patterns of differentiation of
ES cells.[15] But one potential problem seemed to find at least the
hope of a solution in the other major development in embryo
technology, mammalian cloning.

The problem in question is the threat that transplanted tissues derived from ES cells would suffer the same difficulties that
other types of transplant do. Would the host body reject the
transplant, coming as it did from an alien organism? If so, the

promise of stem cell therapy might be considerably diminished. But in Dolly, the cloned sheep, supporters of this research believed they had found a viable solution.

Prior to Dolly, the several attempts to clone mammals had resulted in nothing but failure, and many scientists doubted that cloning was even possible. But Dr. Wilmut's new technology, Somatic Cell Nuclear Transfer, was a surprising success. Dr. Wilmut removed the nucleus (which contains the chromosomes) from a sheep ovum. He then took the nucleus from a cell of Dolly's parent sheep and inserted it in the enucleated egg. Stimulation of the egg resulted in the egg's dividing in the way a normal embryo would. The Dolly embryo was one of twenty-nine embryos that Dr. Wilmut attempted to transfer to sheep uteri, and the only one to survive; as a clone, Dolly was genetically virtually identical to the parent sheep from which the original nucleus was taken—a kind of later identical twin of her parent.[16]

It is this feature of cloning that provokes much optimism among supporters of ESC research. For cloning seems to be the answer to the problem of tissue rejection in transplants. If the embryonic stem cells were obtained from embryos that had been cloned from the patient needing the transplant, the problem of tissue incompatibility would seem to have been solved.

The convergence of these two technological developments—the production of embryonic stem cells and the cloning of Dolly—are largely responsible for the wave of enthusiasm for the use of human embryos as research materials that has shaped the last ten years of debate on the subject. Combined with promises of cures for vicious diseases, expanded life spans, and even the improvement of the human species, the new technologies have captured the imagination of many who have perhaps not looked closely enough at what these procedures entail: a willingness to treat the youngest and most vulnerable members of the human family as disposable objects to be produced and destroyed to benefit others.

In consequence, the pace of technological "progress" has run ahead of moral reflection. Rather than a serious discussion about the nature and value of human embryos, governments have lately been willing to authorize and fund human embryonic research over the protests of many. As mentioned, both California and New Jersey now actively promote embryonic research. And the nation of South Korea was recently sent into a frenzy of excitement with the news of several advances in human cloning and stem cell research by Dr. Hwang Woo-suk; this excitement quickly evaporated, however, when it was revealed that many of these advances involved fabricated data, fraudulent claims, and dubious research.

Meanwhile, prophets of the new cloning revolution, and the attendant genetic revolution, see opportunities to remake the species, including its natural dependence on sexual reproduction. Lee Silver, a biologist at Princeton, whom we will meet again in these pages, foresees a time when advances in genetics make possible stronger, smarter, "enriched" humans, and when advances in biotechnology make possible children who are biologically related to two parents of the same sex or even three or more parents.[17] No "advances" of this sort will occur without a considerable amount of research involving the taking of embryonic human lives. But, as we shall see, the attitudes toward the value of human life in its early stages on the part of these champions of "progress" is morally problematic.

ARE THERE ALTERNATIVES?

The main purpose of this book is to make the positive case for the moral standing of the human embryo, to argue, that is, that it is morally wrong and unjust to kill that embryo, even if the goal of the embryo killing is the advancement of science or the development of therapeutic products or treatments. But it is important to note, if only in passing, two points often overlooked in the debate.

The first is that the promises of the proponents of embryo research are speculative. Moreover, these promises are often exaggerated and unrealistic. When the actor Christopher Reeve died some years after his tragic riding accident, it was suggested by some that opponents of embryonic research were somehow responsible for his death. Similar claims were made when President Reagan finally succumbed to Alzheimer's disease. Such claims are at best wildly inflated rhetoric, and at worst dishonest attempts to manipulate the public argument.

Not only are the benefits exaggerated, but the perils are swept under the rug as well. As mentioned above, the path by which embryonic stem cells become differentiated is not even dimly understood.[18] And even if "normal" development were achieved in a lab, there is little to guarantee that such development would be replicated among all the complexities of the human body. Proceeding under such conditions of uncertainty will involve risk to whatever human subjects are offered the benefits of this research, a consideration hardly ever mentioned.

The second point is that an alternative to some or perhaps all of the therapeutic uses of embryonic stem cells is even now being pursued. Adult stem cell therapies have several decided advantages over possible embryonic stem cell therapies. For starters, they have an established track record of success. For example, bone marrow stem cells are routinely used in the treatment of some forms of cancer. And some scientists believe that adult stem cells might be reprogrammable back to a pluripotent stage, from which they could be directed toward multiple functions. Other scientists have found evidence that some adult stem cells already are at least multipotent (capable of forming multiple cell types) and may be induced to full pluripotency (able to form all the cell types of the adult body). Since adult stem cells are often extracted from the patient in need of therapy, the issue of donor rejection is typically moot. And finally, adult stem cell research does not involve the one inevitably controversial aspect of embryonic stem cell research: it does not require the destruction of human embryos.

This last point would seem a decisive consideration for any society seeking a morally sound resolution of a highly divisive political conflict. For, on the one hand, if federal funds are used to assist in embryonic research, millions of citizens will feel deeply alienated from a society that entangles them in activity they believe to be morally repugnant, and for uncertain gain at best. Adult stem cells, by contrast, offer an alternative that promises benefit to many who are ill, knowledge to the researcher, and a quiet conscience for all citizens.

Nevertheless, most scientists, including some who oppose embryo killing, consider embryonic stem cell research to be a scientifically interesting and medically important realm of inquiry. They are confident that embryonic cells or their equivalent will prove to be profoundly useful in understanding cell interactions and emerging patterns of developing multicellular organisms, including human beings. Furthermore, the pluripotent nature of embryonic stem cells raises the possibility—though it is a speculative one—of an even wider range of therapies than adult stem cells promise. Thus, efforts have been made to find non-embryo-destructive alternative sources of stem cells that possess precisely the qualities of embryonic stem cells. In the final chapter of this book, we return to the question of alternatives to embryo-destructive research, to assess the morality of some of these recent proposals.

RELIGION AND REASON

A morally sound politics would seem to require serious attention to the ethical concerns about embryo-destructive research that responsible commentators on the issue have raised. And yet the argument heard most frequently about what good democratic politics demands makes a different claim altogether. For what is asserted time and again by the proponents of this research is that the convictions of those opposed are guided entirely by religious sentiments. And for this reason, those convictions are ruled out of court as inadmissible evidence for the pro-embryo cause.

On occasion, the claim that the opponents of embryonic research are illicitly religiously motivated even becomes an accusation of bad faith or intellectual dishonesty, particularly when the accused are in fact working from a basis of scientific evidence. Consider, for example, the following, from Lee Silver:

> Those who equate human embryos with human beings invariably believe that each early human embryo is endowed individually by God with a soul or spirit. For those

who hold this belief, it is ensoulment rather than sentience that defines a human being. However, not all religions or religious people abide by such beliefs, and narrow religious arguments are not sufficient to achieve legal and political goals in our pluralistic country. Thus it becomes politically expedient to conjure up scientific-sounding arguments to support what is fundamentally a religious belief.[19]

Professor Silver's claim that those who disagree with him about the humanity of the embryo are acting, not on the basis of considered scientific judgment, but out of "political expediency," and are "conjuring up" arguments that are merely "scientific-sounding," is an insult to the many honorable people, including men and women working in embryology and related fields, who, after looking at the facts, have drawn entirely reasonable conclusions at variance with those favored by Professor Silver. For a scholar to make such allegations without evidence—indeed, as we shall show throughout this book, in defiance of the evidence—suggests that perhaps he is the one not engaging in scientific analysis. Indeed, the use of such terms and phrases as *political expediency*, and so on, amounts to a kind of philosophical name-calling. Its effect is to distract from the real issue at hand, namely, the scientific question of when the life of a particular human being begins, and the moral import of the scientifically established answer to this question.

But doesn't the principled opposition to the destruction of the early embryo rest upon even more disputed propositions of religion and revealed faith about ensoulment, or upon the doctrines of faith traditions opposed through history to abortion and contraception? It does not.

In point of fact, the concept of "soul" will not make an appearance through the rest of this book. Nor will premises from revelation or religious authority play any role whatsoever in the argumentation to follow. As it happens, both authors of this book are dubious of the claim that religion is a purely private matter that should have no bearing on public affairs or even on a citizen's participation (as a voter or officeholder) in public life. But our position in this book is that claims based in religious traditions or revelation are simply not necessary (and probably are not even sufficient) to arrive at correct understandings of embryo science, technology, and ethics.

That is to say, we can know from science what the embryo is,[20] just as we know from embryo technology what can be done to and with it. But we can know from philosophically informed reasoning what it is morally permissible to do to human embryos, and how it is morally impermissible to treat them. Human embryo ethics is, in this regard, no different from the ethics of our treatment of minorities or dependents. Human beings are capable of understanding, through reason, that it is morally wrong and unjust to discriminate against someone because he is of a different race or has a different ethnic heritage. And we are capable of understanding that it is wrong and unjust to discriminate against someone because of his or her age, size, stage of development, location, or condition of dependency.

Human beings are perfectly capable of understanding that it is morally wrong and unjust to treat embryonic human beings as less than fully human. We need religion to support such claims in this domain no more than we need religion to support claims of racial justice or the rights of the disabled. (But again, as the history of the civil rights movement should surely make clear, it would be a mistake to exclude religious voices from arguments about serious moral issues. The civil rights movement, as the abolitionist movement before it, would have been much the weaker without religious leadership playing a prophetic role.)

There are, in consequence, no grounds at all for ruling out arguments of the sort we present in this book from playing a role in public deliberation and public policy. Indeed, if we consider once again the hypothetical story presented earlier of organ harvesting from retarded children, we see how abominable it would be to accuse opponents of such abuses of "playing politics" or "forcing their religious views upon others." Opponents of the killing of the retarded for their organs would only be serving the deepest values on which this nation was established—the *equal* right to life, liberty, and the pursuit of happiness of all human beings.

THE COURSE OF THE ARGUMENT

We argue in this book that embryonic human beings deserve full moral respect. To deny this, one must deny one of four claims. Our book is organized so as to dialectically engage each of these denials.

First, one can deny that the early human embryo *is* a human being. We have already provided some important evidence that confounds this denial, and we will provide much more in chapter two. In chapters six and seven we will address the claim made by some supporters of embryo-destructive research that because early-stage embryos can split into identical twins, they are not yet individuals or determinate human beings.

Second, one can deny that *persons*, the sorts of beings reading this book, are to be identified with the biological entities that are human beings. On this view, ordinary persons like those reading this book are not, despite appearances, living human organisms. Perhaps they are only souls occupying a body; perhaps they are epiphenomena of the material processes of the body; or perhaps they have some other mysterious existence distinct from, and only attached to, the organic bodily existence they seem to have. But they are distinct from that organic body, and therefore need not have existences concurrent with that body's existence. They might, for example, only come into being considerably later than the beginning of the human organism with which they are associated.

Chapter three of this book will make the case that human persons are organisms of a certain type, namely, animal organisms bearing a rational nature. All such organisms—all whole, living members of the species Homo sapiens—are persons. Human beings are special—they have a personal life, characterized by reason and will; but that special life is also a bodily life that begins at conception. Metaphysical self-body dualism, as we shall call it, is false. Human persons are not consciousnesses (or souls) inhabiting and using subpersonal human bodies.

The third way to deny that embryonic human beings deserve full moral respect is to deny that all human beings deserve full moral respect. To be worthy of full respect, someone might argue, a human being must have attained or acquired some qualities or features (beyond merely being human) that is the touchstone of full moral worth. Respect is not owed, in this view, to human beings because of what they *are*. The language of personhood appears again in this debate, not as describing what we humans *are*, but as describing a stage that most (but not all) of us go through, and that many of us also pass out of before dying. One is a person in a way that one can be a child, or a professor—only for a part of one's life. In this view, there are prepersonal and postpersonal human beings, and even human beings (such as severely retarded individuals) who are not, never were, and never will be persons.

We call this view moral dualism, and argue in chapter five that it, too, is false. Some obligations are owed to human beings because of what they have achieved, or because of status bestowed by society—American citizens can vote only when they are eighteen, and immigrants must have citizenship conferred upon them before they can vote. But some obligations are owed, and thus some rights obtain, by virtue of the kind of entity or being one is. These obligations and rights, such as the obligation not to kill and the right to life, are more basic than any of the conferred or achieved rights.

Our arguments in chapter five against moral dualism depend upon claims about ethics that we defend more generally in chapter four. There we argue for an ethical view that has two distinct features. First, it is person-centered. Unlike an ethic that urges promotion of the "greatest good for the greatest number," even when such a good requires the destruction of innocent human lives, the ethic we defend upholds moral absolutes, including inviolable human rights. But second, it is, unlike much Kantian ethics, oriented toward human well-being and flourishing. This ethic, articulated in chapter four, thus helps to show how the moral dualism addressed in chapter five is fundamentally misguided.

These considerations would seem, in sum, decisive against the destruction of human embryos for research purposes. Yet some thinkers attempt to make the claim that, appearances to the contrary, we can both respect the embryos in the way they deserve *and* use them in research involving their destruction. A crucial claim in such arguments is that the embryos in question—the "spare" embryos left over from their creation for reproductive purposes—are destined to be destroyed anyway. So nothing is lost, or there is no cooperation in wrongdoing, if, rather than letting them go to waste, we make use of them for the greater good. We address this type of argument in the second part of chapter seven.

We then draw our conclusion in chapter eight: on the basis of the arguments we have presented throughout the book, it is morally impermissible to engage in any research, for any purpose, that involves the destruction of human beings at any stage of their lives, including the embryonic stage, or in any condition, however weak or dependent. Although it is not the primary purpose of this book, we briefly outline some of the political conclusions that we believe follow from this position. We also return to the question of morally licit alternatives to embryo-destructive research.

We live in a difficult age. Convictions once widely shared about the value of unborn human life have been eroded over the past forty years, especially following the Supreme Court's decision in *Roe v. Wade*. Moreover, intense excitement about the possibility of new knowledge and better health creates incentives that make it difficult to think clearly about our obligations to others, especially when those others are very small, utterly defenseless, and do not look or seem "like us." Competition between nations for scientific prestige and slogans about the march of progress make it seem all but inevitable that embryo-destructive science *will* go forward, without the benefit of sustained moral reflection regarding its ends or its means.

But people who care about justice and human rights should stand fast in the defense of all innocent human life. We hope that the moral reflection we invite people into by presenting our arguments in this book will help them to do just that.

CHAPTER 2

The Facts
of Embryology

. . . . . .

THE CRUCIAL QUESTION

In the previous chapter we briefly looked at some of the recently developed embryo technologies. Through IVF, lab technicians can bring sperm and egg together to produce a human embryo. Through cloning procedures such as Somatic Cell Nuclear Transfer, scientists will likely be able to make a new human embryo that is genetically virtually identical to his or her parent. And through techniques of stem cell technology, we can remove cells of the embryo that, the current evidence suggests, can be cultured to become every type of specialized tissue of the mature human body.

But what are the scientific facts about the early embryo? The answers to this question are often presupposed by those who develop new embryo technologies, and those technologies can help to answer some questions about embryogenesis. But it is helpful to distinguish embryo technology from embryo science, or embryology—the scientific study of what the early embryo is, what it does, and how it develops in its particular way. As we argued in chapter one, embryo science should also be distinguished from moral philosophy and from religion. Moral philosophy (or a religious tradition) might have something to say about how one ought to treat the human embryo. But embryology tells us the facts about the human embryo.

We are concerned in this chapter with what embryo science has to say, ultimately, about the *origins* of human beings. By this, we do not, obviously, mean to ask when the human species, or human life in a generic sense, arose. And so our question is not answered by talk of the continuity of human life through the last few millions of years. We are instead concerned with the origins of individual human beings—human beings like those reading this book, right now. This is the crucial question: when did those human beings begin to be, and what were the characteristic features of their growth and development?

GAMETOGENESIS

Let us consider a particular adult human being, Smith. When did Smith begin? It is a particularly striking feature of human biology, as of mammalian biology generally, that the immediate biological building blocks that went toward Smith's creation were themselves in preparation from the time that Smith's two parents were two weeks old . . . in the womb.

Smith began, if he was not the product of cloning (or, as we shall see, twinning), when a *sperm* cell of his father penetrated and fertilized the *oocyte*, or egg, of his mother. The sperm cell and the egg cell are called *gametes*, or sex cells, and the process by which the gametes came to be developed and formed, called *ga-*

metogenesis, in preparation for Smith's conception, began when Smith's father and mother, respectively, were embryos.

In the case of both developing embryos, during the second week *primordial germ cells* developed and migrated to a yolk sac; they then migrated back to the gonadal region of the embryo at about four weeks. These primordial germ cells are not themselves sperm cells and oocytes, but they constitute the basis from which all further sex cells in the human being will be derived.[1]

From this point, *spermatogenesis*, or the development of sperm in the male, and *oogenesis*, the development of ova in the female, proceed somewhat differently. In the male, the intermediate precursor cells to sperm cells are called *spermatogonia*. "At puberty, the seminiferous tubules mature and the germ cells differentiate into spermatogonia."[2] Spermatogonia give way to *primary spermatocytes* by the process of cell division known as *mitosis*. Each primary spermatocyte, by contrast, undergoes the two-stage process of *meiosis*, the first stage of which produces *secondary spermatocytes*, the second of which results in *spermatids*, which eventually mature into full sperm cells, with heads containing their nuclei, and tails to facilitate mobility.

It is necessary to say a bit more about mitosis and meiosis before turning to the process of oogenesis. Each *somatic* cell of an adult human body (and by "somatic cell" we mean all body cells except sex cells, which are also known as "germ cells") is alike in containing, as we mentioned in chapter one, a genetic makeup identical to the rest of that body's cells. Development proceeds through a process of ever more complex differentiation of specialized cell types that result from different patterns of gene expression, each cell type having its own characteristic pattern. As development proceeds, every cell of the body continues to carry all the genetic information contained by all the other cells, but in each cell only a part of that information is "active." William Hurlbut suggests the useful analogy of a thousand lights that work together to form a sign. The message is determined by which lights are turned on and which are off. In a somewhat analogous way, the pattern of gene expression makes a similarly dramatic difference in the specialized functions that characterize each distinct cell type.

Genes are themselves parts of larger structures called *chromosomes*. Each normal somatic cell contains twenty-three pairs of chromosomes, or forty-six total. One chromosome of each pair comes from the father, and one from the mother. The primordial germ cells of the human being also normally contain forty-six chromosomes. In most cell division, DNA of those chromosomes duplicates itself before the cell divides, and the resulting two cells each possess the full twenty-three pairs of chromosomes for a total of forty-six. This division is called mitosis, and the resulting cells are called *diploid*, to indicate that they contain two sets of chromosomes, making a complete set of forty-six chromosomes.[3]

In every somatic cell, the twenty-three chromosomes from the father and the twenty-three chromosomes from the mother form a complete complement of forty-six chromosomes. Twenty-two of the chromosomes from each parent are essentially identical in configuration. The other pair, the X and Y, however, dramatically differ from each other. Under ordinary circumstances, the forty-six chromosomes of a cell are not easily distinguishable, but are rather in a kind of chromosomal stew or mush. But at both mitosis and meiosis, homologous pairs of chromosomes—one from each parent—condense and pair up. The two homologous chromosomes[4] are truly a perfect match:

"Both chromosomes of each pair carry genes controlling for the same inherited characters. For example, if a gene for eye color is situated at a particular locus on a certain chromosome, then the homologue of that chromosome will also have a gene specifying eye color at the equivalent locus."[5]

At the same time that homologous pairs are meeting, each chromosome doubles its single *chromatid* and becomes a double chromatid chromosome. Biologists call the second chromatid of each chromosome its *sister* chromatid. So early in mitosis a cell has forty-six double chromatid chromosomes, lined up in matched pairs. In mitosis, the two sister chromatids come apart, and the new single chromatid strands move to opposite ends of the cell. Each end of the cell now contains all the genetic material necessary for a somatic cell. New nuclei can form as the single cell divides into two new daughter cells, each with forty-six single chromatid chromosomes.

If a new human being is a result of the meeting of two cells from differing genetic sources, however, then the gamete cells must be somewhat different from the rest of the parents' somatic cells; they must have only one chromosome from each pair. In other words, they must have only twenty-three chromosomes, for the result of fertilization must be a new organism whose cells are themselves in possession of only forty-six chromosomes each. So the primordial germ cells must undergo, in developing into gametes, a different form of division, meiosis, the upshot of which is a sperm or egg cell with a reduced number of chromosomes (twenty-three). Gametes are thus *haploid*, containing half the chromosomes possessed by diploid cells.

Meiosis is itself a two-stage process. In sperm, the process begins with the same matching up of homologous pairs found in mitosis, and the same doubling of chromatids. At this pairing-up stage, there is also *crossing over*: strands of the paternal sister chromatids overlap with strands of the maternal sister chromatids and exchange gene segments. This has as a long-range consequence increased genetic diversity, as each single chromatid after crossing over will be genetically different from the others. Typically, the exchange is for equivalent amounts of DNA; when the exchange is unequal, genetic abnormalities result.

At this point in the cell, there are again four chromatids in each homologous pair, as in mitosis. But in the subsequent two divisions, the resultant four sperm cells end up with only twenty-three single chromatid chromosomes. In a first division, the homologous pairs separate; and in a second, the sister pairs separate. Thus, when a sperm cell penetrates and fertilizes an oocyte, the twenty-three chromosomes of the sperm cell and the twenty-three chromosomes of the egg cell can line up to result in the full forty-six chromosomes of the normal human somatic cell.

As the preceding implies, female germ cells also undergo a process of meiosis. However, in women there are some notable differences. First, unlike sperm, which develop at puberty, and continue to develop throughout adulthood, current evidence suggests the entire supply of the *primary oocytes* is already present in a girl by the time she is born. These primary oocytes, which number around one million at birth, have already begun their first meiotic division, but then go into a dormant stage until puberty.

At that time, the primary oocytes, in monthly succession, once again continue to grow. They are surrounded by the *zona pellucida* and then, in turn, by *follicular cells*. Each month, as the primary oocyte grows, the follicular cells mature; shortly before ovulation the first meiotic division is complete, resulting in the secondary oocyte. Unlike sperm, which emerge four at a time from the process of meiosis, in oogenesis, the end result of the two stages will be only one oocyte. At the division that concludes the first stage of meiosis, most cytoplasm is distributed to the secondary oocyte, while a second cell, the smaller *polar body*, contains little, and eventually degenerates.

Follicular cells are induced to grow by two hormones, the follicle stimulating hormone (FSH) and the luteinizing hormone (LH). At the midpoint of a woman's menstrual cycle, a surge of LH causes ovulation, the release of the secondary oocyte from the woman's ovaries. Shortly before ovulation, the nucleus of the secondary oocyte begins the second phase of meiosis; but it will complete this phase, and shed a second short-lived polar body, only if it is fertilized by a sperm.

For this to happen, the secondary oocyte must be released from the ovaries, where it is developing, and progress down the fallopian tube. At the end of its journey, it will (if intercourse has occurred) be met by perhaps a hundred sperm that have managed to swim successfully to the fertilization site—of approximately two hundred million initially deposited at ejaculation in the vagina.

The preceding description is but a cursory look at some of the events that lead up to fertilization, and some of the main contributors, especially sperm and oocyte, in those events. Much more could be said; in particular, the role of a wide variety of hormones and enzymes has been left unstated for purposes of simplicity.[6] But it is worthwhile to make two points before moving on to a description of fertilization, one of less, the other of greater importance.

The first, and less significant, was briefly alluded to earlier. To trace the biological developments that eventually resulted in our friend Smith coming into being, we need to go all the way back to the beginning of Smith's parents' lives. From the outset, those two young human organisms are preparing for what, from the standpoint of biology, is surely one of the most important events of an organism's life—its reproduction. Each human embryo is not just busy with his or her own growth and development but is already laying the groundwork for the growth and development of his or her descendants. This proves little, in terms of the overall goals of this book, of course; but it is a remarkable window into the complexity of human life in its earliest days.

The second point is crucial. What *are* the sperm and the oocyte, biologically speaking? That is, are gametes like little parasites, independent organisms inhabiting the bodies of adult human beings? Or are they perhaps, as once was thought of sperm, proto or miniature human beings, which will, upon entering the uterus, begin to grow and develop? Is either the sperm or the oocyte, or both together (though they are physically apart), identical to Smith, the adult whose origins we wish to specify?

The answer to all these questions is negative. Sperm and egg cells are parts of the human organism, the sperm a part of the male, the egg a part of the female. We should not be misled by the fact that sperm have, for example, tails, can swim, and can even survive for a time inside the female. Fixed location within an organism is neither necessary nor sufficient for something to be a part of an organism. Rather, a part of a biological organism in the sense that concerns us here is some living subset of the cells that comprise the totality of the organism, the life of which subset is integrated into the life of the whole, and which performs some unified functional role within the life of the organism. Because their unified functional role demands an appropriately unified structure, parts may be studied independently of the organism of which they are parts; indeed, we may study the parts of parts of organisms. (Since cells have parts, which are not themselves cells, our definition is not to be considered exhaustive; but all the parts we are concerned with at this point are composed of at least one cell.) But parts do not have the independent existence that individual wholes have; while they may continue to live briefly when separated from the organisms of which they are parts, and may be artificially maintained, they typically cease to be shortly after separation.

So hearts and blood cells are both parts of organisms, for they are sets of cells whose life is bound up with the life of the whole organism, and which play a unified functional role in the organism's life, and which have, accordingly, a unified structure. Dead fingernails, and pacemakers, by contrast, are not parts of organisms. Dead fingernails are no longer integrated into the life of the human being; and pacemakers never were, and never will be, integrated into that life. Pacemakers, even if placed within the body, remain outside the biological matrix that is the organism's life, though they play an important extrinsic role in helping the organism to maintain its own life. Similarly, a parasite such as a tapeworm has its own life, separate from that of its host, and plays no supportive functional role within the organism's life. But, like hearts and blood cells, sperm and egg are best understood as parts. Even the life span of sperm and egg are limited, and relative to their functional roles. If fertilization is not accomplished, the oocyte typically ceases to be within twenty-four hours after ovulation; and sperm degenerate within two to five days.

If sperm and egg are simply parts of the organisms in which they are found, then clearly neither is identical with Smith, who is a complete human individual, a biological whole. Nor is either identical to the embryo that results from fertilization. As a part of recent philosophical and political polemics in favor of embryonic research, it is sometimes claimed that sperm and egg have as much a claim to identity with the later organism—Smith— as does the fertilized egg, or embryo. But this is certainly false. For, as we shall now see, that embryo is itself a whole human individual—it is not a part of anything.

FERTILIZATION

The oocyte, which is usually fertilized in the *ampulla* of the uterine tube, where it is widest, possesses, after ovulation, two structural barriers to sperm. The first is called the *corona radiata*, which is composed of follicular cells; the second is the zona pellucida, a glycoprotein shell surrounding the egg. Enzymes must be released both to facilitate sperm progress through the corona and then the zona, and to block further penetration once one sperm has entered the plasma membrane of the oocyte. (Polyspermy, the fertilization of the egg by more than one sperm, is a source of significant abnormalities, forming either disorganized nonembryonic entities, or severely damaged, nonviable embryos.)

Sperm too must undergo a change called *capacitation* before they are ready to penetrate the egg. This process, by which a "glycoprotein coat and seminal proteins are removed from the surface of the sperm's acrosome," leaves the mature sperm more active than before, and capable, as it was not before, of fertilizing the egg.[7] Prior to in vitro fertilization, discussed in chapter one, sperm must be capacitated in a chemical bath before they can be brought into contact with the oocyte.

Once the sperm has penetrated the zona, the oocyte completes its second meiotic division, which results in a second polar body and a definitive oocyte. The nuclei of both the mature oocyte and of the sperm now begin to enlarge, becoming, respectively, the *female pronucleus* and the *male pronucleus*. Both pronuclei, which contain all the chromosomal material of the sperm or egg, replicate their DNA in anticipation of the one-celled embryo's first mitotic division, called cleavage, and the male pronucleus moves closer to the female pronucleus.

When does the zygote—the new human organism—come into being in this process? Some embryologists hold that the next stage of fertilization marks the definitive moment. Male and female pronuclei join. Recall that as part of the formation of gamete cells, and the oocyte's second meiotic division, the number of chromosomes characteristic of the human cell was reduced from forty-six to twenty-three in the male and female pronuclei. When those pronuclei come together, the twenty-three chromosomes from the male and the twenty-three from the female unite, resulting, William Larsen writes, "in the formation of a zygote containing a single diploid nucleus. Embryonic development is considered to begin at this point."[8]

Fertilization, as used to describe the transformation of two parts, sperm and egg, into a single entity, the human embryo, is certainly complete by the time the two sets of chromosomes have intermingled. The zygote is now genetically unique and its sex is established. Both features are a result of the haploid nature of the gametes, and their subsequent fusion. This fusion brings about a combination of chromosomes that includes both maternal and paternal DNA. In addition, in the first phase of meiosis, as mentioned, crossing over of the chromatid segments of the paired chromosomes has resulted in further genetic variation among the gamete cells. In consequence, the newly formed zygote is genetically distinct from either of its two parents.

While these claims provide a persuasive case for the claim that the zygote comes to be *no later* than at *syngamy*, i.e., the lining up of the twenty-three pairs of chromosomes, we are inclined to think that the definitive moment occurs even earlier, once the sperm has entered and united with the oocyte. Once this has happened, both sperm and oocyte undergo such significant changes that neither seems to exist in its own right anymore. The sperm breaks up on entering the oocyte, and, other than its nucleus, is largely dissolved. The oocyte also undergoes fundamental changes, as its zona hardens, to prevent polyspermy, and it completes its second meiotic division. We no longer, in consequence, have two distinct organic parts, sperm and egg, each with a distinct identity.

At the same time, when sperm and oocyte cease to be, there now appears to be a distinct organism directing its own processes of growth and development, processes that include the lining up of the maternal and paternal chromosomes at syngamy, as well as the processes just described of hardening the zona and completing the second meiotic division. The first process especially seems characteristic of a new organism, whose existence depends upon a structural barrier to outside forces, rather than of a gametic cell, whose existence is fundamentally oriented toward *uniting* with another gamete, and thus does not have an impermeable external barrier. For these reasons, we think it most likely that the definitive moment marking the existence of a new human organism is fertilization, defined as the union of sperm with oocyte.

It is important to be clear what is at issue here. The question that needs to be asked is: When is there a single biological system with a developmental trajectory, or active developmental program, toward the mature stage of a human being? That is a question for which there is, in principle, a definitive scientific answer. We are suggesting that the answer to this question is: shortly after the union of sperm with oocyte. Some people believe it happens slightly later. However, there is widespread agreement among embryologists both that a new human individual comes into existence when there is a single, unified, and self-integrated biological system, and that this happens no later than syngamy.

Among the twenty-three chromosomes possessed by each gamete, one, the sex chromosome, determines whether we have a boy or a girl. The oocyte always possesses an X sex chromosome; sperm may possess an X or a Y chromosome. When the result of fusion is an XX combination, the zygote is female; when the result is XY, the zygote is male. So, by the time the chromosomes have lined up, the sex of the embryo is already settled.

Keith L. Moore and T. V. N. Persaud, in *The Developing Human*, summarize what has happened:

> *Human development begins at fertilization* when a male gamete or sperm (spermatozoon) unites with a female gamete

or oocyte (ovum) to produce a single cell—a *zygote*. This highly specialized, totipotent cell marked the beginning of each of us as a unique individual. The zygote, just visible to the unaided eye as a tiny speck, contains chromosomes and genes (units of genetic information) that are derived from the mother and father. The unicellular zygote divides many times and becomes progressively transformed into a multicellular human being through cell division, migration, growth, and differentiation.[9]

Earlier, we asked whether the sperm and the egg were best characterized as parts of an organism or independent organisms. We answered that they are parts: they do not have an independent existence from the mother and father, and in fact serve a functional role, for which they are equipped with adequate structural features. This functional role is determined in relation to the needs of the organism of which they are a part, and in particular, in relation to the need to reproduce. Can the same be said of the zygote? Is it, too, simply a part of the organism within which it now resides?

No. The newly formed zygote is genetically different from its parents. Of course, sperm and egg cells were genetically different as well; but this genetic difference—their haploid rather than diploid nature—is itself a structural feature that reflects functional demands: the new human being (assuming no serious abnormality) must have forty-six chromosomes with genetic information from both parents, so the sex cells, whose job it is to unite to form the new human being, must have only half the usual complement of chromosomes. This haploidy of the gamete cells distinguishes them from whole human beings. The zygote, by contrast, is genetically complete. Its genetic difference is not a matter of genetic absence, as is a gamete cell's genetic difference from the other diploid cells of the organism of which it is a part. It has all the genetic information it will need to develop and grow into a much larger organism.

Moreover, the zygote does not itself serve a functional role in the biological economy of either parent; it is a separate organism, distinct and whole, albeit at the very beginning of a long process of development to adulthood. If it is provided with the resources needed by all organisms, namely nutrition and a reasonably hospitable environment, it will continue (assuming adequate health) to grow and develop. Moreover, its growth and development is, from this point, determined from within. It contains within itself the "genetic programming" and epigenetic characteristics necessary to direct its own biological progress. It possesses the active capacity for self-development toward maturity using the information it carries.

Nicanor Austriaco expresses several key points:

> The egg is a cell, an embodied process in stasis that only has the life expectancy on the order of hours because it is not self-sustaining. It is unable to meet the energy demands needed for survival. In contrast, the embryo is an organism, an embodied process that has a life expectancy on the order of decades precisely because it has the capability to sustain itself as an independent entity. It is a dynamic system which arises from the necessary interactions among the mix of molecules that is created by the fusion of the

egg and the sperm, and it manifests itself as the visible and morphological changes which we call human development.[10]

In short, there are profound differences between the sperm and egg, on the one hand, and the newly formed zygote, on the other. We will return to the question of the nature of the zygote later in this chapter, and, in particular, to our claim that it is a whole, living individual of the human species. For the moment, however, it is necessary to continue the discussion of the biological development of the embryonic human being.

THE FIRST WEEK: CLEAVAGE AND IMPLANTATION

The newly formed zygote is not yet in place in the uterus, where it will receive maternal nourishment and grow for the next nine months. It must first make a journey to the uterus. Along the way, it begins, at a rather leisurely pace, its first processes of biological development. Yet for much of its first week, prior to implantation in the uterus, it does not actually grow in size.

Rather, it undergoes a number of cell divisions referred to as *cleavages*, in which the resulting cells are progressively smaller, and enclosed within the zona pellucida. Its first cleavage is from one cell to two. Subsequent cleavages are asynchronous. First one of the two cells divides; there are now three cells. Then the second cell divides to result in a total of four cells. These cells of the embryo are called *blastomeres*.

At about the eight- to ten-cell stage, the blastomeres undergo a process of *compaction*. As this word suggests, the blastomeres change their shape and become tightly aligned. Moore and Persaud write of compaction that it "permits greater cell-to-cell interaction and is a prerequisite" for later specialization of cells.[11] By three days after conception, the embryo contains around sixteen cells, and looks something like a blackberry. Hence its name at this stage, *morula*, derived from the Latin word for *mulberry*. At this stage, the morula has an inner group of cells, called the inner cell mass, and an outer cell layer.

At four or five days, the morula-stage embryo enters the uterus, and the distinction between inner and outer becomes more pronounced. A fluid-filled space called the *blastocyst cavity* separates the embryo into two quite distinct parts. The first, a thin outer layer called the *trophoblast*, is the progenitor of the placenta. The inner cell mass, called the *embryoblast*, "gives rise to the early embryo proper."[12] The whole embryo at this point is now referred to as a blastocyst.

Over the next two days, the zona pellucida degenerates, and the embryo eventually pierces a hole in it, from which it exits the zona membrane. This is called *hatching*. No longer constrained, the embryonic human then grows rapidly. Six days after fertilization, "the blastocyst attaches to the endometrial epithelium [the uterine lining]."[13] This begins the process of implantation; "by 10 to 12 days after fertilization, the embryo is completely embedded in the endometrium."[14] By the beginning of this process, the embryo has begun taking in nourishment from surrounding maternal tissues. Embryologists believe that early embryos often fail to implant; the result is a very early spontaneous abortion likely to be mistaken for an unusually heavy menstrual period.[15]

THE SECOND WEEK

Further development of the embryo can be treated relatively quickly. Much of the second week after fertilization is still concerned with implantation, which is not completed until day ten to day twelve. In addition, much of the morphological change concerns the formation of extraembryonic structures, such as the amniotic cavity and amnion; the primary and secondary yolk sacs; the connecting stalk and the chorionic stalk. Implantation makes it possible for the embryo to receive oxygen and nutrition from the mother. The various structures necessary for providing the new individual with a suitable environment and adequate nutrition are in place early in human development.

In the meantime, however, there is some development of the embryo proper, although it is largely preparatory to much greater changes in the third week. This development is heavily dependent on the activity of the trophoblast. The cells of the trophoblast send specific biomolecular signals to the cells of the inner cell mass which in turn promote their further development. Two changes are particularly important.

The first is the division of the inner cell mass into a two-layered embryonic disc (in the third week, a third layer is generated by a process known as gastrulation). This disc "gives rise to the germ layers that form all the tissues and organs of the embryo."[16] In addition, in one of the two layers, the *hypoblast* (the other is the *epiblast*) the "prechordal plate [develops] . . . which indicates the future cranial region of the embryo and the future site of the mouth; the *prechordal plate* is also *an important organizer of the head region.*"[17]

THE THIRD WEEK:
GASTRULATION AND NEURULATION

Let us imagine we are looking down upon the embryo from above at the beginning of its third week (roughly the fifteenth day from fertilization). On both the top and the bottom, the embryo is sandwiched between two fluid-filled cavities, the amniotic cavity on the top, and the yolk sac on the bottom. Imagine, though, that we have removed the amniotic cavity and are now looking at the two-layered embryonic disc. In its third week of life, the embryo will develop a third layer through the process of *gastrulation*. The embryo proper now has three primary germ layers (the *ectoderm*, the *endoderm*, and the *mesoderm*), and will begin to manifest early neural structures through *neurulation*.

As we are looking down upon the top (dorsal) part of the embryonic disc, it is shaped something like a serving platter—slightly oval. What will happen over the next week is that the embryo will elongate, with one side becoming the clear precursor to the head, the other the rump. The former side of the embryo is called its cranial side, the latter its caudal side. From the caudal to the cranial sides, structures will develop that will become the vertebral skeletal structure of the developing embryo.

The process of gastrulation begins with a migration of cells to the center and back of the embryonic disc. Again, keeping our serving-plate image in mind, on one side of the plate we should see a ridge emerge from the back edge of the plate extending toward the middle on the top layer of cells, or the *epiblast*. This is the *primitive streak*. From the beginning of the primitive streak, we now have a way of identifying the front end of the embryo (it is on the side opposite to the primitive streak) and the right and left sides of the embryo.

The primitive streak is additionally important in terms of the concerns of this book. Once the primitive streak has begun, cell destination becomes much more rigidly determined. Prior to the emergence of the primitive streak, cells are sufficiently un-committed to specialized roles that, when disrupted (biochemi-cally or mechanically), twinning is possible. As we mentioned before, evidence suggests that at the very earliest stages even sin-gle cells or clumps of cells can be detached from the embryo and develop as ordinary embryos. But until the formation of the primitive streak, it is possible for the embryo as a whole to divide. Each new embryonic whole is now capable of developing toward the mature stage of a human being. The result, of course, is identical twins. (Fraternal twins are a result of the fertilization of two eggs by different sperm.)

Twinning is important for us in this book because it plays a crucial role in a family of arguments used by supporters of embryo-destructive research that assert that the early human embryo is not a single individual substance, but a mere mass of cells, so long as twinning is possible. Because twinning ceases to be generally possible around the time of the development of the primitive streak, many embryo-research proponents say this should be the marker past which destructive research should not be allowed.

We think these arguments fail, and shall say why in chapter six. It is worth pointing out here, however, that were these argu-ments sound, then the emergence of the primitive streak would mark the emergence of the human being himself or herself, for human beings are individuals; if there is no individual substance prior to gastrulation, then there is no human being. But this flies in the face of everything that embryology tells us about the early embryo. Thus, as we have seen, Moore and Persaud write that the initial totipotent cell that is the result of fertilization "*marked the beginning of each of us as a unique individual* (italics added)."[18] William Larsen writes that male and female sex cells "unite at fertilization to initiate the embryonic development *of a new individual.*"[19] Ronan O'Rahilly and Fabiola Müller state that "*a new, genetically distinct human organism* is formed when the chromosomes of the male and female pronuclei blend in the oocyte (italics added)."[20]

All these embryologists and developmental biologists, who are collectively responsible for the standard textbooks in their fields, agree in marking fertilization, not gastrulation, as the beginning of a human individual. As we have said, it will be important to address philosophical claims about the alleged nonindividuality of early human embryos in chaper six, but readers should take note here that such claims are certainly not the norm among the work of scientists specializing in human embryology.

To return now to gastrulation, many cells from the epiblast (the top layer of the embryonic disc) migrate through the primitive streak and go on to form a new layer of cells. As a result, the embryo now has the form of a three-layered disc consisting of ectodermic cells, facing up; endodermic cells on the bottom; and mesodermic cells in the middle. Cell location in each layer again plays a crucial role in determining what parts of the human being a cell will help to develop.

The primitive streak extends toward the middle of the embryo until about eighteen days, at which time a different line of cells, the *notochord*, emerges. Bruce Carlson summarizes the nature of the notochord.

> The notochord . . . is a cellular rod running along the longitudinal axis of the embryo just ventral to the central nervous system. Although . . . it serves as the original longitudinal support for the body, the notochord also plays an extremely important role as a prime mover in a series of signaling episodes (inductions) that transform unspecialized embryonic cells into definitive tissues and organs [including] . . . the conversion of overlying ectoderm into neural tissue.[21]

The notochord is crucial to neurulation, the formation of the nervous system, or, more precisely, the formation of the neural plate and neural folds, which close to form the neural tube. The notochord induces the formation of the neural plate, which gives rise to the brain and spinal cord. Moore and Persaud describe the process of neurulation:

> As the notochord elongates, the neural plate broadens and eventually extends cranially as far as the oropharyngeal membrane [this provides the source cells for the mouth]. Eventually the neural plate extends beyond the notochord. About the eighteenth day, the neural plate invaginates along its central axis to form a longitudinal median *neural groove*, which has neural folds on each side. The *neural folds* become particularly prominent at the cranial

end of the embryo and are *the first signs of brain development.* By the end of the third week, the neural folds have begun to move together and fuse, converting the neural plate into a *neural tube*, the promordium of the CNS [the brain and spinal cord].[22]

Again, looking down on the dorsal surface of the embryo, what we can see, moving from cranial to caudal ends, is the area in which the brain will develop, and the axis along which the vertebral skeletal structure will develop.

By the end of the third week, the embryo has gotten itself ready to enter the next four-week phase of intense structural development, the period known as *morphogenesis*, or development of form. Tissue and organ systems undergo considerable development in these next few weeks; but all such growth was made possible by the various types of development we have seen in the early embryo over the first three weeks.

WHAT IS THE EARLY HUMAN EMBRYO?

Further development of the embryo and fetus will be familiar to many, especially those who have glanced through a pregnancy handbook. All the major organs have formed by the eighth week, at which time the embryo has taken on a distinctively human appearance. However, rather than continue to describe the growth and development of the early human being from this point, we wish to summarize what we take to be the major conclusions to be drawn from the evidence. We will return to many of the claims we make in this section in other chapters, to defend them against philosophical challenges. But we think everything we say in this section is amply supported by the facts we have recounted about embryogenesis.

There are three important points we wish to make about the human embryo. First, the embryo is from the start distinct from any cell of the mother or of the father. This is clear because it is growing in its own distinct direction. Its growth is internally directed to its own survival and maturation. Second, the embryo is human: it has the genetic makeup characteristic of human beings. Third, and most important, the embryo is a complete or whole organism, though immature. The human embryo, from conception onward, is fully programmed and has the active disposition to use that information to develop himself or herself to the mature stage of a human being, and, unless prevented by disease or violence, will actually do so, despite possibly significant variation in environment (in the mother's womb). None of the changes that occur to the embryo after fertilization, for as long as he or she survives, generates a new direction of growth (except in the case of twins, which we discuss below). Rather, all of the changes (for example those involving nutrition and environment) either facilitate or retard the internally directed growth of this determinate and enduring individual.

Here, then, is the bottom line: A human embryo is not something different in kind from a human being, like a rock, or a potato, or a rhinoceros. A human embryo is a whole living member of the species Homo sapiens in the earliest stage of his or her natural development. Unless severely damaged or denied or deprived of a suitable environment, an embryonic human being will, by directing its own integral organic functioning, develop himself or herself to the next more mature developmental stage, i.e., the fetal stage. The embryonic, fetal, child, and adolescent stages *are just that*—stages in the development of a determinate and enduring entity—a human being—who comes into existence as a single-celled organism (a zygote) and develops, if all goes well, into adulthood many years later.

In chapter one, we looked at some recently developed reproductive techniques, such as in vitro fertilization and human cloning. If the embryo is produced by either of these two means, is it still a human organism?

Let's first take the case of an embryo produced by in vitro fertilization. The embryo, which is the product of the union of male and female gametes, just as in ordinary sexual reproduction, is a single, individual human organism, albeit one that is brought into existence outside of the natural environment it needs to survive. Occasionally, a very sloppy claim is made that because the embryo in a petri dish cannot (unless transferred to a uterus) grow into a mature human being, it is therefore not a human being. Such a claim has no scientific basis. A petri dish is simply not an appropriate environment in which an embryo can grow past a very early stage. Similarly, the moon or the Antarctic is not an appropriate environment for an adult human being to live in without technological support. All human beings are dependent on their environment for their ability to grow, survive, and flourish, and human beings early in their development are no exception. Embryos produced in vitro are certainly human beings.

But what if the embryo is produced by cloning, rather than by the union of gametes? Is a cloned human embryo a subhuman organism? The answer is surely no. Just as fertilization, if successful, generates a human embryo, cloning, if successful,

produces the same result by combining what is normally combined and activated in fertilization, that is, the full genetic code
plus the ovular cytoplasm. Fertilization produces a new and complete, though immature, human organism. The same is true of
successful cloning. Because cloned embryos are the same as other
embryos, they ought to be treated as having the same moral status, whatever that might be, as other human embryos. We will return to the case of cloned human embryos in chapter seven, in
order to respond to Paul McHugh, a member of the President's
Council on Bioethics, and a proponent of the claim that cloned
human embryos—*clonotes*, as he labels them—are not human
beings.

Human embryos possess the genetic and epigenetic pri-
mordia for self-directed growth into adulthood with their unity,
determinateness, and identity fully intact. As the (hypothetical)
story, recounted at the beginning of this book, of the adult Noah
looking back on the events of his life illustrated, the adult human
being is the same human being who, at an earlier stage of his or
her life, was an adolescent, and before that a child, an infant, a
fetus, and an embryo. And even in the embryonic stage, that human being was undeniably a whole, living member of the human species.

We argued earlier that none of this is true of the gametes
that joined in sexual reproduction. Neither male nor female sex
cells are whole, distinct organisms. They are functionally, struc-
turally, and genetically identifiable as parts of the male or female
(potential) parents. Each has only half the genetic material
needed to guide the development of an immature human being
toward full maturity. They will either combine with an oocyte or

spermatozoon to generate a new and distinct human organism, or simply die. Even when fertilization occurs, they do not survive; rather, their genetic material enters into the composition of a new organism.

But consider how different this is from the case of the human embryo, from the zygote and blastula stages onward. The combining of the chromosomes of the sperm and the oocyte generates what every authority in human embryology, as we have seen, identifies as a new, distinct, and enduring organism. Whether produced by fertilization or by Somatic Cell Nuclear Transfer or some other cloning technique, the human embryo possesses all of the genetic material needed to inform and organize its growth. The direction of its growth is not extrinsically determined, but is in accord with the genetic information within it. Moreover, unless deprived of a suitable environment or prevented by accident or disease, the embryo is actively developing itself to maturity. Thus, it not only possesses all of the necessary organizational information for maturation, but it truly possesses an active disposition to develop itself using that information. The human embryo is, then, a whole, though immature, and distinct human organism—a human being.

If the embryo were not a complete organism, then what could it be? Unlike the spermatozoa and the oocytes, it is not merely a part of a larger organism, namely the mother or father. Nor is it a disordered growth, such as a hydatidiform mole or a teratoma.[23] Such entities lack the internal resources actively to develop themselves to the next more mature stage of the life of a human being. Their direction of growth is, like a cancer, not toward maturity.

Perhaps someone will say that the early embryo is an inter-mediate form, something that regularly emerges into a whole (though immature) human organism, but is not one yet. We will encounter such claims in chapter six. Yet what, to anticipate our later argument, could cause the emergence of the whole human organism, and cause it with regularity? It is clear that from the zygote stage forward the major development of this organism is controlled and directed from within, that is, by the organism it-self. So, after the embryo comes into being, no event or series of events occurs that could be construed as the production of a new organism. That is, nothing extrinsic to the developing organism itself acts on it to produce a new character or new direction of growth.

Sometimes people object if we say that human embryos are human beings, on the grounds that they have the potential to become mature humans, the same will have to be said of sperm and ova. But the objection is untenable. As we have shown, the sex cells are not whole or complete organisms; the early em-bryo is.

Nor are human embryos comparable to somatic cells, like skin cells or muscle cells, as some have suggested. Like a male or female gamete, a somatic cell is functionally only a part of a larger organism. It does not contain within itself the internal re-sources and active disposition possessed by the embryo to de-velop itself to its full maturity. The gene expression pattern of the nucleus of a somatic cell may be transformed by the process of Somatic Cell Nuclear Transfer, so as to produce a human em-bryo. But such a change must come from without; skin cells never, by internal self-direction, develop into human embryos. No skin cell possesses an active disposition to use the genetic information within it to develop itself toward maturity as a complete and separate member of the species.

So a human zygote, embryo, or fetus is not something other than a human being. He or she is not an individual of some other or intermediate kind of species. Rather, the human zygote, embryo, or fetus is a human being at a certain (early) stage of development. When, then, did this human being begin to exist? The evidence that we have given supports only one conclusion: the vast majority of us came into existence by no later than the end of fertilization, by which point it is clear that a new, human organism exists, distinct from his or her mother and father.

It is necessary to add the qualification "the vast majority of us," because there are exceptions to this claim about the beginning point of human beings. For identical twins do not come into existence at fertilization. At least one twin comes to be at a later point when the embryo divides—probably because of some extrinsically caused disruption—into two genetically identical human beings. What has happened to the early embryo? Some think that the early embryo is identical to one of the subsequent twins; it is as if a new embryo has "budded" off from the first. Others think that the first embryo ceases to be, and two new embryos take its place. In either view, however, it is clear that at least one embryo comes into existence at a stage later than fertilization.

For this reason, it is necessary to enter the qualification "the vast majority" when discussing the beginning of a human being's existence. But this qualification has no bearing on the following point, which also follows from the evidence we have marshaled thus far: when someone destroys a human embryo, it is a human being that is killed. This is true of any embryo, from the end of fertilization on: every human embryo is a human being; there-fore, ending an embryo's life is ending a human being's life, even if that embryo may give rise to twins.

Someone might grant that an embryo is a human being, yet distinguish between human beings, considered as complete hu-man organisms at any stage of human development, and human persons. Perhaps persons are souls, or minds, or forms of con-sciousness. In this view, not all human beings (the unborn) are yet persons, and some human beings (the senile, the brain damaged) are no longer persons, and some human beings (the seriously re-tarded) will never be persons. Perhaps you, the reader, and we, the authors, are mistaken in identifying ourselves as human be-ings. This raises the philosophical issue to which we turn in chap-ter three, "Who, and what, are *we*?"

CHAPTER 3

Dualism and Persons

. . . . . .

WHAT WE ARE

What are we? Are we human beings who began to exist when sperm and egg united to produce a new, complete, and distinct human organism—a new human individual? Or are we something else, something other than, though somehow related to, the bodily creature that (for example) seems to be reading this book right now? Did you, the reader, or we, the authors of this book, come to exist sometime after the complete human organism that each of us seems to be came into existence? Are we something distinct from what seem to be our bodily selves? Are we nonbodily "persons" (independent souls, minds, consciousnesses, or what have you) who "inhabit" or reside in or somehow "supervene on" nonpersonal bodies?

There are various ways to ask these and related questions. We could, for example, ask about the kind of *substance* that we humans are. Or, meaning the same thing, we could ask about our "nature," or our "essence." Some have suggested that the use of the language of *substance, essence,* or *nature* in debates about human embryos is unhelpful or archaic, but we disagree. When we speak of substance or nature or essence, we are drawing attention to a distinction between the *kind* of thing an entity is and the various properties or characteristics that an entity might possess accidentally, contingently, or temporarily.

Consider an oak tree in your backyard. There is an obvious difference between what kind of entity it is—an oak tree—and its accidental properties—the properties, for example, of being in your backyard rather than in your neighbor's, of being seventy-five rather than ninety feet tall, and of having an upright posture rather than a slight stoop or crookedness. For the entity in your backyard would cease to exist if it ceased to be an oak tree, but it would not cease to exist if your neighbor purchased the plot on which it stands, or if it grew fifteen feet, or its upright posture was compromised. Indeed, through all these changes, the oak tree would remain not only an oak tree, but the very same oak tree. Because of the kind of entity the oak tree is—we could say because of its substance or essence or nature—this particular oak tree will continue to exist, through its various changes, as an oak tree. It will cease to exist as an oak tree only when it dies (i.e., it ceases to exist).

Similarly, consider a dog, Rufus. Rufus began to exist when this particular dog began to exist, and he will cease to exist when this particular dog ceases to exist. But he did not begin to exist when he began to run, or when he grew teeth, or when Smith purchased him; nor will he cease to exist if he ceases to possess the traits of running, having teeth, or living in Smith's house (and shedding on Smith's couch). Rufus belongs to the substance kind "dog," and possesses accidents such as running, having teeth, or having hair. We clearly mark this difference in our ordinary speech. When we are asked what Rufus is, we answer not that he is something with teeth, or something walking, but that he is a dog.

Of course, some of the properties Rufus has, or that the oak tree has, are not accidental, but are related to their substantial kind. Both, for example, are alive, and neither would continue as a dog or an oak, respectively, if it ceased to be alive. Our understanding of the nature of an entity seems, in fact, to proceed by a recognition of the difference between its accidental properties and those properties that together characterize it as the sort of thing it is.

Nor are its essential properties characteristics that must be on display at all times, or to the same degree: oak trees develop certain (oaky) properties, and live oaky lives—oak trees do not grow maple leaves, and they certainly do not chase cats. But young oaks do not yet have any leaves, and a withered or deformed oak may not have as many, or as healthy a set of, leaves as a flourishing oak. But it is because the oak tree has a particular nature that it develops, in its time, and in its way, a certain range of properties natural to the sort of thing it is.

Now we are concerned in this chapter with a question about the readers and authors of this book, and all the other beings that are the kind of substance we are, whatever that substantial nature might be. What is our substance kind, our nature, our essence? What sorts of beings are we, substantially, rather than accidentally? We will argue in this chapter that we are, in fact, living organisms of the human species, that is, we are human beings. Such a position seems to be the height of commonsense thinking; when you look in the mirror, you see a member of the species Homo sapiens, and you recognize that human individual as yourself. Yet many philosophers have denied this historically, and many continue to deny it. They insist that we are not human beings, but something else.

What other sort of entity could we be? Most philosophers are rightly impressed with certain properties shared by the readers and authors of this book, that are not shared by dogs or oaks: we possess reason—the ability to think critically, abstractly, and logically—and the ability to choose—to make decisions based on reason, rather than following mere blind impulses. The readers and authors of this book are also self-conscious, and are clearly language users. So philosophers and others, in various ways, have often thought that these properties, and only these properties, were the essential characteristics of a kind of being that we could call a "person."

Now, we do not wish to deny that we are persons. Later in this chapter, we will briefly show how the fact that we are human beings is to be squared with the fact that we are persons; briefly, in the same way that oaks live oaky lives, human beings live personal lives—lives characterized by a certain range of potentialities, which need not be fully instantiated or realized all at once or to the same degree in all cases. In chapter four, we will discuss the moral importance of our being persons—persons have inherent dignity, and the lives of persons are intrinsically valuable; thus persons may not be deliberately killed. But we think it a grave mistake, in recognizing these truly special properties we possess, to fail to see that we are also *essentially* bodily, organic beings, part of the physical world, with biological lives essential, not accidental, to our existence.

Among the areas in which the gravity of this mistake is

most clearly seen is in the area of embryo ethics. For embryos clearly cannot yet think, choose, and speak; nor are they (yet) self-conscious or even sentient. Were this to mean that embryos were not the same *kind* of beings as the readers and authors of this book, that they were not *persons*, then it would be difficult to see why they should be accorded the same moral respect that we, authors and readers, believe we are entitled to. There would be no obvious reason why they should not be destroyed for the sake of beings who really are persons. And thus would be opened a clear path to experimentation on human beings at early developmental stages.

We will argue, then, in this chapter, that we, the readers and authors of this book, and all other beings essentially like us, are in fact human beings, the same kind of entity that we showed human embryos to be in chapter two. To do this, however, we need to explain, and then refute, the philosophical claim about persons and human beings known as "dualism."

DUALISM

Dualism is a many-headed beast; there are a variety of forms, depending upon what one thinks the entity other than the human being, but with which we are supposed to be identical, really is. In this section, we identify several general types of dualism. Of these, all but the last are the sort with which we are concerned in this chapter—we can call them all forms of ontological or metaphysical dualism. The last, which will be the concern of chapter five, we will call moral dualism. Ontology and metaphysics are concerned with what sorts of things really exist; morality is concerned with how we should act. So metaphysical dualism differs from moral dualism in making a claim about what sorts of things exist, and not just a claim about how we should act toward those things that exist.

What all forms of metaphysical dualism have in common is the identification of a kind of being with which we are identical, but which is substantially different from the human organism. For simplicity, we will often give this entity the name *person*; hence most forms of metaphysical dualism can be identified by the generic name "person-body dualism." But the nature of the personal entity differs somewhat from theory to theory.

MIND-BODY
AND SOUL-BODY DUALISM

In the history of philosophy, two figures have stood out for the importance and influence of their dualistic views, Plato and Descartes. Plato advocated a soul-body dualism, Descartes a mind-body dualism.

In Plato's dialogue *Phaedo*, Socrates described his attitude to his impending death:

> [W]hile we are in the body, and while the soul is mingled with this mass of evil, our desire will not be satisfied, and our desire is of the truth. For the body is a source of endless trouble to us . . . [and] if we would have pure knowledge of anything, we must be quit of the body. . . . In the present life, I reckon that we make the nearest approach to knowledge when we have the least possible concern or interest in the body, and are not saturated with the bodily nature, but remain pure until the hour when God

himself is pleased to release us. And then the foolishness of
the body will be cleared away and we shall be pure and
hold converse with other pure souls.[1]

Plato believed that the soul preexisted its stay in the body
and, if it did not become entirely corrupted by the body, it would
continue to live immortally afterward. Because he regarded the
soul as our true nature, and was opposed in various ways to the
needs and desires of the body, Plato advocated a strong separation in way of life from the body, a separation practiced only by
the true philosopher. Thus Plato held that philosophy was truly
the practice of dying, a way of preparing for the longed-for lib-
eration of the soul from the body.

René Descartes, by contrast, in his *Meditations on First Philosophy*, argued that there are two fundamental substances: extended substance, or body, and thinking substance, or mind.
Because we know that we are thinking substances, yet it is possible, Descartes said, to conceive of thinking substance as existing
without extended substance, we must conclude that the true person is thinking substance, to which extended substance is closely
aligned, but of a different nature. Descartes' language is very
similar to that which we have used to discuss the difference between substance and accident, but his conclusion is quite different:

. . . from the fact that I know that I exist, and that meanwhile I judge that nothing else clearly belongs to my nature
or essence except that I am a thing that thinks, I rightly
conclude that my essence consists in this alone: that I am
only a thing that thinks. Although perhaps . . . I have a

body that is very closely joined to me, nevertheless . . . it is therefore certain that I am truly distinct from my body, and that I can exist without it.[2]

Both Plato and Descartes thus identify the true self, or person, with an immaterial entity that is substantially different from the body proximate to that entity, and indeed, is capable of a separate existence.

Some religious conceptions likewise hold that the souls of the dead continue to live after the death of the body. For this reason, some have inclined toward dualism, to identifying the person with the soul that can live separated from the body. Some Christians, historically, and in the present day, have believed that human beings are souls living, for now, in bodies, but their bodies are distinct from their true selves (i.e., their souls). There is, however, contrary to this, a strong tradition of Christian thought that holds that the soul is not identical to the person, but an animating principle of a unified being, i.e., of a true body-soul composite. Thus, Saint Thomas Aquinas wrote that if only my soul were to survive the death of the body, then *I* should not, for "the soul is not the whole human being and my soul is not I."[3] Thus, Christianity's continued emphasis on the resurrection of the body does not seem consistent, in the end, with Platonic or Cartesian forms of dualism.

·

LOCKEAN DUALISM

Many recent thinkers hold to a form of dualism that does not explicitly identify the person with a separate immaterial entity. Rather, the person is identified as the subject of consciousness, or self-consciousness. John Locke held such a view. A person, he wrote,

> ... is a thinking intelligent Being, that has reason and reflection, and can consider itself as itself, the same thinking thing in different times and places; which it does only by that consciousness, which is inseparable from thinking, and as it seems to me essential to it.[4]

Now one might think, as we do, that all this is true of human beings—true, at least, of those who have developed their natural potentialities to the appropriate stage. But Lockean dualism holds that these properties must be actively possessed, or be (more or less) immediately exercisable for there to be a person at all. So persons are *separate* entities from their bodies, and come to be only when an entity more or less immediately capable of reason and reflection begins to exist.

BRAIN-BODY DUALISM

This Lockean "person" seems to be a somewhat mysterious entity; can nothing more be said about the locus of consciousness, or its relation to the organic body? Believing that souls, minds, and even persons are too immaterial to be compatible with contemporary philosophical materialism, some people today say that the person is identical to his or her brain.[5]

Such a view is implicit in some philosophical accounts of the origins of the person that holds that persons do not come into existence until a brain develops, and that also hold that a *different* substantial biological entity precedes the existence of the brain. These views are similar to Plato's and Descartes' in their emphasis on the "minded" nature of persons, but holding, as they do, that minds are brains, they are committed to a brain-body dualism. Jeff McMahan articulates (and defends) this view:

> . . . we do not begin to exist until approximately 28 to 30 weeks after fertilization—assuming that current estimates of when in the course of fetal development consciousness becomes possible are roughly accurate. This, of course, is well after our organisms begin to exist.[6]

McMahan does not believe that the brain is a substance capable of independent existence, of course, but a part of an organism. Yet, because his theory separates what we are—the brain—from the animal organism that begins earlier than the brain, it seems fair to categorize his view as a species of dualism.

Brain-body dualism is not always explicitly articulated. Many philosophers prefer simply to speak of "the person I am" as distinct from "my body" without identifying what sort of substance that person is (apart from the claim that it is a personal substance, of course). But for those who, for whatever reasons, embrace materialism, the most plausible material substance with which to identify the "self" or the "person" seems plainly to be the brain.

CONSTITUTIONALISM

Recently, the philosopher Lynn Rudder Baker has defended a view of persons as distinct from their bodies that she calls the "constitution" view.[7] Baker argues that the relation of constitution, which is the relation in which human animals stand to human persons, is not that of identity. It is possible for x to constitute y and also possible both that x might not have constituted y, and that x might cease to constitute y. However, it is the case that under the appropriate circumstances, x necessarily constitutes y.

To take an example of Baker's, a piece of cloth, shaped and designed in a certain way, under some circumstances constitutes a flag. But the cloth is not identical to the flag, even though it makes sense, using the "is" of constitution, to say that this piece of cloth is a flag—this flag. For, apart from the appropriate circumstances, this cloth might not have constituted a flag at all. For the cloth to be a flag requires, e.g., a state, that the cloth has been made by the right persons, with the intention of making a flag, and so on. Similarly, the cloth could cease to be a flag under the right circumstances, which are presumably various. Although the cloth is necessarily a flag—necessarily constitutes a flag—under the appropriate circumstances, it is not intrinsically necessary that this cloth constitute a flag. It can precede and postdate the existence of the flag that it sometimes constitutes. So the cloth cannot be identical to the flag.

Baker's view of the human person runs along similar lines. A human person is constituted by, but not identical to, a human animal. The same animal precedes the person, and often exists after the destruction of the person, and under the appropriate circumstances, necessarily constitutes the human person. But if the animal had been destroyed prior to coming to constitute a person, then that animal would have existed without the person—any person—ever having been constituted by it.

Baker's view differs from both mind-body and soul-body dualism, for, as the cloth-flag analogy makes clear, there is not a separate and independent entity that is identical to the person. And her account is somewhat less vague than the Lockean personhood view, since she attempts to specify philosophically the nature of the organism-person relationship. Still, her view is dualist: the organic body is not itself a person in its early stages, and often is not in its later stages either. Moreover, Baker believes that the person who is constituted by the organic body might come to be constituted by a different body, even a nonorganic body such as a machine. Such claims are clearly dualist.

MORAL DUALISM

We here briefly describe a final type of dualism, which we will discuss at greater length in chapter five. This type is not metaphysical—it does not hold that there is some type of entity that persons are that is different from the human being. Rather, it treats personhood as a stage or a phase through which human beings may come and go, like student, or adolescent.

The entry (and exit) requirements for "being a person"—i.e., for entering or existing in the person stage of one's existence—differ from thinker to thinker. For some, personhood is socially bestowed; for others, it comes with a certain level of cognitive achievement. But personhood is generally taken by such thinkers to be the state a being must achieve or attain in order to merit moral respect. On this view, therefore, while it might be true that the readers and authors of this book and all other humans came into being in the embryonic stage, they did not become worthy of moral respect until some later stage of development.

THE TROUBLE WITH DUALISM

Let us begin our critique of person-body (or "self-body") dualism by providing a brief road map of the arguments we will advance against it.

We will first note the commonsense reasons for thinking that we are unitary beings—that is, that both our minds and our bodies are aspects of one unified entity, rather than independent substances. We also identify some of the problems that historically have plagued dualist accounts, such as Plato's and Descartes'. We will then offer three philosophical arguments against dualism, and for the view that we are unitary substances.

The first argument, which has roots in the thought of Thomas Aquinas, is directed against a common dualist assumption: that the subject of mental acts is different from the subject of bodily acts. Our argument is based on the unity of perception and understanding and shows, again, that bodies and minds, or consciousnesses, are parts of one unified entity.

The second argument shows that any view that conceives of the person as an entity separate from the biological organism requires deeply problematic metaphysical claims in describing what the relationship is between the two substances, one organic, one personal.

Our third argument was first put forth by Germain Grisez, and later developed by him with Joseph Boyle and John Finnis. This argument shows that dualism is inherently irrational. The dualist cannot coherently assert the dualist position to be true, because he or she has nothing stable to assert it to be true of.

By this point, dualism will have been shown to be a lost philosophical cause. Yet dualism is perennially attractive. After providing our arguments against dualism, we ask why this is so; Lynn Rudder Baker, we believe, gives a very clear statement of what many believe to be the great difficulty with the claim that entities such as the readers and authors of this book—persons, all of them—are, essentially, human beings. Baker suggests that it runs contrary to reason to think of human animals as persons. We will say why we think the very opposite is true.

Thus not only will dualism be shown to be untenable, a competing view will emerge as reasonable and defensible. What, then, shall we call our competing view? The view that we argue for in this book and especially in this chapter is that we are human animals. Following recent work in the philosophy of personal identity, we shall call this view "animalism," or the "animalist" view. Animalism is true, we hold, and, in conjunction with the findings of chapter two, it justifies the following inference: for the vast majority of us—all those who were not the products of monozygotic twinning (i.e., twinning from a single fertilized egg)—we began to exist at conception: the point at which a new and distinct individual of the species Homo sapiens came into being as a complete, living human organism.

OUR ANIMAL LIVES

Why is it natural to think of ourselves as human animals, rather than some other sort of substance that merely inhabits a human organism? This question is important, because we hold that the animalist view is not simply a bit of metaphysical speculation, but is true to how we experience ourselves and our relations to other persons and to the world. For we experience ourselves, at a very commonsense level, as bodily beings.

Thus, when we run or walk, we do not think of our body as bringing us someplace, but of ourselves as going someplace. When we meet a new person, we do not think of the exchange as an interface of two bodies, mediating the communication of two persons who cannot touch or directly communicate with each other. Rather, in seeing the other's face we think we have seen the other him- or herself. And we think this of ourselves as well; when we look in the mirror, we believe that we see a reflection of ourselves.

A dualist such as Plato or Descartes is inclined to separate the mind or soul from the body, and thus to distinguish the inner self from the outer body. By contrast, the philosopher Wittgenstein once said that the best portrait of a person's soul was his body. This remark shows the close connection between internal and external, between our inner sense of self and our outer presentation of self; this strong connection is effaced in dualistic accounts.

The connection is similarly effaced as regards the nature of human action. When I wish to eat an apple, I reach out and take it; I then take a bite. Thus, I see, reach for, touch, and taste the apple. In all these actions, consciousness—mind—and body are fully integrated. My seeing is not like the inner presentation of a picture. My reaching out does not consist of an inner attempt, and then an external reach. Nor do touch and taste consist of an external sensation and then an internal one. Internal and external are integrated in all these happenings.[8]

This separation of the inner world of experience from the outer world of concrete realities is responsible for some of the most important objections to dualism that have been raised over the centuries. For example, in Descartes' dualistic account, knowledge of the external world becomes deeply problematic. If I am a mind, then the impact of the external world on my body in, for example, sight is not an impact made by the world on me. So the effect made by the world upon the body must then in turn be made upon the mind by the body.

Now it is mysterious how substances of such putatively different natures as minds and bodies can have causal impacts upon one another; but it is equally problematic to assume that whatever mental representation I have of the world as a result of the body's causation really is accurate to the world. For the Cartesian dualist, the mind is at such a distance from the world that knowledge begins to seem impossible. Thus many philosophers have believed that an immediate consequence of Descartes' dualism is the problem of knowledge, and the inevitability of skepticism.

Our first argument against dualism is somewhat similar to this historical difficulty. However, rather than assuming that dualism is true, while revealing an insuperable difficulty with dualism, it takes as its starting point our natural way of experiencing the world, described earlier, and argues from this to a claim about the unity of the human being in experience and understanding.

The metaphysical dualist holds that subjects of consciousness are different sorts of entities than are bodily subjects. But this is shown to be false by returning again to the sorts of actions that we perform, actions like reaching for an apple or riding a bike. If a living thing performs bodily actions, then it follows that it is a physical organism. If Robert P. George (henceforth RPG), one of the authors of this book, is riding a bike, then what he should, and does, rationally say, think, and believe is: "I am riding a bike." The subject of the action, to which "I" refers, is not understood by RPG as being something other than the physical being pedaling along.

Or, consider judgments of sensation, such as, "That is a tree." Sensation is a bodily action. The act of seeing, for example, is an act that an animal performs with his eyeballs and his optic nerve, just as the act of bike riding is one he performs with his legs. But it is clear in the case of human individuals that it must be the same entity, the same subject of actions, that performs the act of sensing, and that performs the act of understanding necessary for forming a judgment. When Chris Tollefsen (henceforth CT), the other author of this book, knows that "That is a tree," it is by an act of the visual sense that he apprehends the tree, which he refers to as "that." But it is by understanding, or a self-conscious intellectual act, that he apprehends what is meant by *tree*, apprehending *what* it is (at least in a general way). CT's judgment—"That is a tree"—however, brings together in one act the objects of both a physical and an intellectual act. Clearly, it must be the same thing—the thing that CT refers to when he says "I"—which apprehends the predicate and the subject of this unitary judgment.

So, it is the same substantial entity, the same agent, that understands and that senses or perceives. And so what all agree is referred to by the word *I*, namely, the subject of conscious intellectual acts, is also identical with the physical organism that is the subject of bodily actions such as sensing and perceiving. Hence the entity that CT is, which he refers to using the word *I*, and the entity that RPG is, which he refers to using the word *I*, and the entities that you, the readers of this book, are (and each of you also refers to yourself using the word *I*) is in each case a human physical organism.

It is, of course, true—indeed, it is central to the argument just presented—that this organism has capacities that are best described as "nonphysical," such as the capacities for consciousness, reflection, and choice. These are capacities that we agree are "personal." So we believe that it is entirely correct to say that we, the authors and readers of this book, are persons. We will discuss, both later in this chapter and in the two to follow, what the relation is between being a person and being a human animal, and of what moral significance it is that we are persons. But the arguments so far show that we are not persons in any sense that divides our personal reality from the reality of the animal organism that began (for most of us) at conception. Rather, the argument so far continues to show that the authors and readers of this book really did begin then.

As mentioned above, some philosophers are less forthright than Plato and Descartes in attributing an independent existence to the person they believe themselves to be.[9] Nevertheless, they hold that persons have particular sorts of essential properties—those properties, as we showed earlier, that an entity must continue to possess in order to stay in existence. Because persons are taken to have some set of psychological properties essentially, it is held that entities of the person sort cannot come into existence before these properties emerge, and that entities of the person sort cease to exist when these properties disappear. The philosopher Eric Olson has recently raised a difficult question for any such position.[10] Olson calls this view the psychological approach. As we will see, Olson's objection is directly relevant to the sorts of questions with which we were concerned in chapter two.

Olson points out that according to the psychological approach, the readers and authors of this book were never, for example, fetuses, for we, readers and authors, are essentially persons, and substances of the person sort do not come to exist until the onset of psychological traits. But fetuses themselves seem to belong to a substance class—they are particulars of the substance sort "human animal." And this raises problems for the view that we are essentially persons. What, for example, has happened to that other substance, the human animal? Does it continue to exist in the same space as the human person? Does RPG, for example, occupy the same space as a human animal? Or did the human animal cease to exist with the coming to be of the human person? When CT began, did he replace the human being that preceded him?

If the former is the case—if RPG shares space with a human animal—how can that animal not share exactly all of RPG's properties, and if so, why is *it* not also a person? If the latter, is there now no longer a human *animal* in the space that CT occupies? Neither of these options seems metaphysically acceptable; it is more reasonable to hold that RPG and CT, like all the readers of this book, are essentially human animals; thus we were all once fetuses, and, given the evidence of chapter two, embryos as well.

So, we have seen that metaphysical dualism and the psychological approach raise impossible-to-answer questions about the relationship between the animal substance and the personal substance; and that commonsense features of our life—our ability to walk, eat, and sense—illustrate the unity of the being who performs these activities. Our third argument against dualism shows that the attempt to speak about dualism while denying that unity is impossible.

Our natural experience of ourselves is as psychophysical

unities; we experience ourselves, and our relations with the world and with other human beings, as "minded bodies," subjects of both physical properties and conscious experience. The dualist attempts to show that the human being is, by contrast, two distinct realities, specifically, a "person" and a subpersonal body. But any such theory must contradict its own starting point, since reflection necessarily begins from one's own conscious awareness of oneself as a unitary actor. It is this being that the dualist sets out to explain, to himself and to others; he takes note of the complexity of his experience, and attempts to give an account of the nature of the being who has these experiences.

But his account begins by dividing the reality of the being he attempts to explain into two realities, the person and the body. Or he identifies one side of the equation as a mind, or a subject of consciousness, or a soul. He sets out to explain one thing, but does so by introducing two. But then, with which of the two entities does the dualist identify himself in presenting his explanation of the nature of the being with which he is concerned? The only two options, of course, are to identify himself with either the spirit, person, subject of consciousness, or mind, on the one hand, or with the organic living body on the other. Grisez, Finnis, and Boyle, however, reveal the deep flaw in either approach:

> . . . if the I be identified with the spirit-person, the living organism recognized by others as the reality whose behavior constitutes philosophical communication is not identical with the person excogitating the reflections communicated. And if the I be identified instead with the living organism whose behavior communicates those reflections, the spirit excogitating the reflections is not identi-

cal with the only reality recognizable as a person communicating them. Spirit-person and mere living human body are philosophical constructs neither of which refers to the unified self who has set out to explain his or her own reality; both of them purport to refer to realities other than that unified self but somehow, inexplicably, related to it.[11]

In other words, *who* is the dualist? The very principles of dualism make it impossible for the dualist to answer this question without making further communication impossible.

HOW ARE ANIMALS PERSONS?

The arguments presented over the past several pages seem to us conclusive to defeat dualism. And in defeating dualism, we believe we have given good reasons for thinking that we, readers and authors of this book, and all other humans are animals. We believe that animalism gives us a true account, as dualism does not, of our nature. Yet dualism is and has been attractive to a number of people, including philosophers. What accounts for this attraction, and how can we respond to it?

Lynne Rudder Baker, in the course of defending her "constitution" view of persons, and criticizing animalism, presents, we think, a very fine statement of the grounds for resisting animalism. These grounds emerge by consideration of our ordinary conception of persons. Of this ordinary conception, Baker writes,

> An adequate account of personal identity over time should have something to do with what is required to be a

person at all. And the pretheoretic concept of a person is the concept of something with psychological states, something that can be a rational and moral agent. It is these person-making features that should determine what counts as personal identity over time.[12]

We agree with Baker. For example, it seems bizarre that something with psychological states, that can be a rational and moral agent, could be a mere body, a lump of matter, as it were. This, in fact, is why we argue that we are animals, rather than (strictly speaking) bodies. Animals are not mere lumps of physical stuff, like a rock or a piece of metal. But Baker suggests that it is equally implausible to think of animals as meeting these criteria:

> If . . . we are most fundamentally animals, *then our uniquely characteristic abilities do not stem from our being the kind of entities that we are.* This is so because on the Animalist view, what we are most fundamentally—human organisms—can exist and persist without [psychological states]. Having a first person perspective, on the Animalist View, is irrelevant to the kind of being that we most fundamentally are.[13]

Baker claims that this is a deep "reason to reject any Animalist criterion" of personal identity. Again,

> [A]n animalist criterion of personal identity over time simply leaves out these person-making features. On the Animalist view, "psychology is completely irrelevant to personal identity."[14]

So how can animalism be squared with the commonsense view of these person-making characteristics?

We should first note that all forms of dualism that, like Baker's, require an entity to possess psychological properties in order to be a person are in a bind from the beginning. For human beings who are in a dreamless sleep, or in a deep coma, seem not to possess the relevant properties. Yet few dualists wish to assert that persons go out of existence in such circumstances.

Rather, dualists typically make the *capacity* for psychological states the criterion for personhood—an entity is not a person if it does not have the capacity for reason, choice, self-consciousness, and so on. And, of course, human beings in the embryonic, fetal, and early infant stages lack immediately exercisable capacities for mental functions characteristically carried out (though intermittently) by most (not all—consider cases of severely retarded children and adults, and the aforementioned comatose persons) human beings at later stages of maturity. Still, they possess in radical (i.e., root) form these very capacities. Precisely by virtue of the kind of entity they are, they are from the beginning actively developing themselves to the stages at which these capacities will, if all goes well, be immediately exercisable.

In this critical respect, early human beings are quite unlike cats and dogs, even fully mature members of these species. As humans, they are members of a natural kind, the human species, whose embryonic, fetal, and infant members, if not prevented by some extrinsic cause, develop in due course and by intrinsic self-direction the immediately exercisable capacities for characteristically human functions. Each new human being comes into existence possessing the internal resources to develop such capacities, and only the adverse effects of other causes will prevent their full development. So in this sense, even human beings in the embryonic, fetal, and infant stages have the basic natural capacity for characteristically human functions of the sort that dualists are rightly impressed by.

So we must distinguish two senses of the capacity (or, as it is sometimes called, the potentiality) for mental functions, psychological states, and so on: an immediately exercisable one, and a basic natural capacity, which develops over time. But if this is so, then there is little mystery in how an embryonic, fetal, or infant human being, incapable at the time of exercising his or her mental capacities, is nevertheless a person: that a human being does, by its nature, have the radical capacity for such mental acts, and is by a self-directed process developing that capacity to the point where it is immediately exercisable.

This is likely to be missed if we fail to view the early human being in its fully temporal existence. If we take a snapshot of the embryo or fetus or infant at some particular stage of development, then we will be inclined to assign it essential properties based entirely on what it has at the moment of the snapshot. But this seems an inappropriate perspective for determining the nature of an animal. Tigers are essentially carnivorous, and, as such, have certain types of teeth and claws. We would hardly be inclined to say that a tiger cub, not yet fully developed, was for that reason not a tiger. And while oak trees essentially are leafy, they do not have leaves at every stage of their lives. By contrast, a piece of cloth that has not yet been made into a flag is in no way a flag. No piece of cloth ever develops itself to the stage of being a flag; all the work of making the cloth into a flag must come from somewhere (indeed, someone) else. External causes act upon a piece of cloth to make it (i.e., transform it into) a flag.

The point is that, keeping in mind what we said early in this chapter about the distinction between substance and accident, organisms such as tigers and human beings do have natures, and those natures manifest themselves in certain essential properties. But because the life of an organism is a life in time, those properties are rooted in capacities of the organism that must develop through time—no tiger or human being springs into being fully formed with all of its capacities developed to the point at which they are immediately exercisable. Body-self dualists look only at the properties essential to human life, such as mental functioning and self-consciousness, as they exist at the height of their development. But where could such properties have come from if they were not already rooted in the nature of the being that possessed them?

So animalism—the view that we are, essentially, human beings, members of the species Homo sapiens—is not only true, but not really in tension with the view that we are also persons. The persons that we are, are not entities separated from our animal bodies; we are neither independent minds, spirits, nor brains. Rather these particular individuals—RPG, CT, and you, the reader, members of the species Homo sapiens—all are themselves persons, have always been persons, and will cease being persons only when we cease to be, by dying.

CONCLUSION

If we are, by our nature, human animals, then it is natural to ask when we began to exist. This question seems definitively answered by the findings and arguments of chapter two. Except in the case of some monozygotic twins, each of us began at fertilization, and even a monozygotic twin who came into being other than by fertilization began as an embryo and then developed normally as a human being.

It is additionally natural to think as follows. If we are by our nature human animals, and human animals live personal lives, then we are, all of us, persons. But if persons, were we not entitled to moral respect right from the start of our existence? If we had been deliberately killed in the zygotic or embryonic or fetal stage (perhaps to obtain cells to be used in biomedical research to help others), would this not have been a wrong against us? Surely the answer is yes.

Nevertheless, serious doubts have been raised about this conclusion, and they deserve to be answered by reasoned arguments. In the next chapter, therefore, we will provide an outline of an ethical framework within which human persons can be shown to be worthy of moral respect from the time they come into existence. We will also show that certain other ethical theories are inadequate. So the conclusion to be reached at the end of the next chapter does indeed validate the natural thought: all human beings, even in the embryonic stage of their lives, are worthy of full moral respect and should not be reduced to the status of disposable research material.

CHAPTER 4

Moral Philosophy
and the Early Human Being

. . . . . .

Ethical theory seeks to identify principles of right action. By the identification of such principles, moral agents are guided in their deliberation about what they may do, must do, and must refrain from doing. Thus ethical theory—moral philosophy—seeks to provide the sort of normative guidance that is essential to answer questions about, among other things, the right treatment of other human beings, including very young human beings, very old human beings, and human beings who, as a result of disease, accident, or genetic defect, are physically handicapped or mentally retarded. For it cannot be doubted that many of our questions—indeed, the vast majority—about how to live and act concern our relations to other human beings.

We pointed out in chapter one that answering these questions is not the domain of science (though scientific knowledge is often critical, as in enabling us to know whether we are dealing with a human being or some other type of creature). This is because science is concerned primarily with questions of fact, questions that concern the way the world is. But the questions we are concerned with here—in particular, questions about the right treatment of human beings at early developmental stages (zygotes, embryos, fetuses)—are not questions about the way the world is. Rather, such questions are, as we said in the previous paragraph, normative: they concern what ought to be the case, how one ought to act, what sorts of things one ought, and ought not, to do.

In particular, we are concerned with the following questions: Is it permissible to experiment upon embryonic human beings for the sake of the benefits, especially health benefits, that might be made available from such experimentation? Could we create embryos for precisely such purposes? Could we use left-over embryos from in vitro fertilization? Is it morally wrong to engage in embryo-destructive research, even if the potential benefits are great? No claim proper to embryo science, or embryo technology, can answer these questions, for the former tells us only what the embryo is, the latter only what can be done to the embryo. We need to discover what ought to be done, and what we must refrain from doing.

There are, of course, different moral theories and philosophies. And of these, some come to different answers to the same moral questions, even, in some cases, when all the facts of the case are agreed upon. This is not to say—far from it!—that the facts are unimportant. Indeed, it is precisely because of the importance of the facts that we spent most of chapter two setting forth certain facts of biology, in particular, the fact that the human zygote or later embryo is a human being in a very early stage of development. And, although it is a "metaphysical" fact, rather than a fact of science, we went on to show in chapter three that self-body dualism is false, and that beings such as the readers and authors of this book are, essentially, human animals. Thus we concluded with a factual claim: we, the authors of this book, and all of the readers who are not the product of monozygotic twinning (or cloning), began at fertilization.

Still, disagreement in ethical theory can persist even in the face of facts such as these. For this reason, it is equally important to ground one's ethical reflections in a sound moral philosophy. And not all moral philosophies are equally sound; indeed, since many such ethical theories contradict one another, at least some of them must be false.

In this chapter, we first discuss a moral theory that we believe to be both false and pernicious: consequentialism. This theory must be discussed, because it is the foundation of much of the contemporary discussion of the ethics of scientific research, and especially research into embryonic human beings. Even people who recognize the humanity of the early embryo, and even people (though less often) who believe that all human beings are persons, might permit lethal experimentation on human beings if strictly guided by consequentialism. So it is imperative to show this theory to be mistaken.

We then turn to a theory that we think is not so much mistaken as inadequate: the deontology of Immanuel Kant. Kant, we believe, identified a central moral truth about the right treatment of human beings, a truth that almost certainly suffices to rule out embryo-destructive experimentation. But Kant's insight can be supplemented, we argue, with the work of thinkers from the natural law tradition.

A natural law theory is, in essence, a critical and reflective account of the constitutive aspects of the well-being and fulfillment of human persons and their communities. Like consequentialism, and unlike Kantianism, it takes the human good to be of central moral concern. Like Kantianism, and unlike consequentialism, it also sees human persons as the central nodes of moral significance. Human persons may not be damaged or destroyed, according to the natural law tradition, for the sake of some "greater good." Indeed, as we will see, the entire notion of a "greater good" is suspect, at least as that notion is deployed by consequentialist ethical theories.

Our natural law theory will propose to identify the principles of right action—moral principles—as specifications of the most general moral principle of morality, the principle that one should always choose and act in ways that are compatible with a will toward integral human fulfillment. And among the principles are respect for the rights that people possess simply by virtue of their humanity—rights that, as a matter of justice, others are bound to respect, and governments are bound not only to respect but, to the extent possible, to protect. So the conclusion of this chapter will be the claim that all human beings, including human beings at the beginning of their lives, have rights that may not be violated, and which must be protected by law, including the right to life. It follows that any person who performs lethal experiments upon early human life, and any state that permits (much less funds) such experiments, is in grave violation of the fundamental rights of the youngest and most defenseless members of the human family.

BENTHAM, MILL, AND SIDGWICK

We distinguish, as do many philosophers, utilitarianism as a moral theory from consequentialism. Consequentialism is broader than utilitarianism, but as a specific theory, utilitarianism came first. Consequentialism proposes to evaluate actions on the basis of which option will produce the optimal (i.e., best possible) consequences. Utilitarianism is a specific type of consequentialism that identifies good and bad consequences wholly or primarily by reference to happiness, often understood as a greater balance of pleasure over pain.

Three of the earliest and most influential utilitarian thinkers were Jeremy Bentham, John Stuart Mill, and Henry Sidgwick. Looking at the areas in which these thinkers agree, and those in which they disagree, gives some idea both of the nature of utilitarianism and of its weaknesses.

Jeremy Bentham makes two important claims at the beginning of *An Introduction to the Principles of Morals and Legislation*. The first concerns the sources of motivation for human action: "Nature has placed mankind under the governance of two sovereign masters, pain and pleasure. It is for them alone to point out what we ought to do, as well as to determine what we shall do."[1] In keeping with this reduction of motives for action to pain and pleasure, Bentham asserts that the fundamental principle of morals and law is the Principle of Utility (which Bentham later came to call the Principle of Happiness).

Bentham writes:

> By the principle of utility is meant that principle which approves or disapproves of every action whatsoever, ac-

cording to the tendency which it appears to have to augment or diminish the happiness of the party whose interest is in question: or, what is the same thing in other words, to promote or to oppose that happiness. I say of every action whatsoever; and therefore not only of every action of a private individual, but of every measure of government.[2]

But Bentham is not simply concerned with utility relative to some individual, but with the utility of the political community. So "An action then may be said to be conformable to the principle of utility . . . when the tendency it has to augment the happiness of the community is greater than any it has to diminish it."[3]

Two points are immediately of importance in Bentham. The first concerns his theory of value. For Bentham, the only values and disvalues are those of pleasure and pain. Happiness is understood exclusively as a balance of the former over the latter. Second, Bentham's ethical guidance for judging action in pursuit of these values is maximizing: the principle of utility enjoins us to pursue the greatest good for the greatest number. So Bentham's utilitarianism is hedonistic—it identifies good and bad with pleasure and pain—and consequentialist—it identifies the best action as the one that maximizes good consequences. While not all forms of utilitarianism or consequentialism adopt Bentham's hedonism, all accept the maximization principle.

John Stuart Mill did not accept Bentham's particular form of hedonism. He argued instead that there were higher and lower pleasures: "some kinds of pleasure," he wrote, "are more desirable than others," and he identified these as "pleasures of the intellect, of the feelings and imagination, and of the moral sentiments."[4] But he did not differ from Bentham as regards the foundational principle:

> I have dwelt on this point [the difference between lower and higher pleasures], as being a necessary part of a perfectly just conception of Utility or Happiness, considered as the directive rule of human conduct. But it is by no means an indispensable condition to the acceptance of the utilitarian standard; for that standard is not the agent's own greatest happiness, but the greatest amount of happiness altogether.[5]

Mill's theory, then, is consequentialist, although he differed about what the goods to be maximized were. But the difference begins to point out one of the central defects of utilitarianism and consequentialism generally, as we see when we turn to Sidgwick.

Henry Sidgwick, the last great nineteenth-century utilitarian, considered in his book *The Methods of Ethics* whether to agree with Bentham or Mill on the question of hedonism. But, while recognizing the attractions of Mill's claims, he adopted psychological hedonism, the doctrine that only pleasurable states of consciousness are valuable, and that there are no intrinsic differences of value as between such states, for a simple reason. Only by adopting this view, Sidgwick believed, could maximization be possible. For if there were values—even pleasures—different *in kind* from one another, then there would be no common standard by which the various possible options for action could be weighed against one another so as to determine which would be in accordance with the maximizing principle.

The difficulty is critical. Bentham's theory of value should strike us as terribly naive and clearly false. It is obvious enough that not all pleasures are good for us; should the pleasures involved in sadomasochistic practices, for example, be considered just as good as the pleasures of ice cream, or of working at a homeless shelter? Further, it is clear that we pursue many possibilities for the good or benefit they promise us, but not because of the pleasure they offer. So those reading this book because they hope to make intellectual headway on arguments about embryonic life, or in order to make better moral decisions in the future, or even because they believe the authors are purveyors of fallacies that must be exposed, are not doing so because they believe it will maximize pleasure. Rather, as we shall argue later in this chapter, they do so because they recognize knowledge, or practical wisdom and integrity in action, as goods by which they may be made better off through their own actions. So Bentham's theory of value seems a hopeless nonstarter.

But Bentham's position, like those of Mill and Sidgwick also, is a maximizing approach to value. And in order to maximize something, there must be a common standard by which to judge which option offers the most, whether it is the most value, the most pleasure, the most mileage, or the most durability. Now it is at least arguable that if we focused on something narrowly called "sensible pleasure" we might find that all such pleasures could be measured against one another, so as to determine, for some possible course of action, which would provide us with the "greatest" amount of pleasure. (Of course, it is also possible that even sensible pleasures are not weighable in this way. As Alasdair MacIntyre notes, "The pleasure-of-drinking-Guinness is not the pleasure-of-swimming-at-Crane's-beach." He concludes on the basis of a consideration of pleasures that "the notion of the greatest happiness of the greatest number is a notion without any clear content at all."[6])

But when we move from this very limited approach, and consider the whole range of genuine goods, including (but not limited to) knowledge, integrity, friendship, health, and aesthetic appreciation, then it is equally clear that there is not a common standard by which they may all be weighed against one another. Mill's attempt to do justice to a more adequate account of value than Bentham allowed for was thus rightly seen by Sidgwick as incompatible with the utilitarian aspiration to a "scientific" ethics of maximization.

UTILITARIANISM
AND CONSEQUENTIALISM

Some later utilitarian and consequentialist theories have attempted to preserve Mill's insight that the nature of value transcends mere sensible pleasures. Such theories continue to be faced with the problem, as we shall call it, of incommensurability: there is no way of commensurating, or weighing, a multiplicity of values of different kinds, all of which offer different benefits and provide different reasons for action.

Other theorists have pursued the commensurating project, without the hedonistic simplicity of Bentham, by identifying preferences or desires as the foundation for the principle of utility: whatever maximizes preference or desire satisfaction is to be pursued, according to such accounts. But these accounts are equally implausible. For, just as there are clearly bad pleasures, there are also clearly bad preferences and desires: why should Hitler's preferences and desires, any more than his pleasures, count equally with the preferences of a Mother Teresa, or a Gandhi? Nor will it do to speak only of one's highest or best preferences, for this will then simply smuggle in moral considerations into the assessment of preferences and desires.

Some utilitarian and consequentialist theorists have attempted to stay closer to Bentham's original formulation. The consequences of this approach to value for morality are, however, quite striking. In Peter Singer's view, for example, utilitarianism is committed to the equal consideration of the interests of all sentient creatures. These interests are to be understood in terms of the creature's ability to experience pain and pleasure. In discussing Bentham's view, Singer writes:

> Bentham points to the capacity for suffering as the vital characteristic that gives a being the right to equal consideration. The capacity for suffering—or more strictly, for suffering and/or enjoyment or happiness—is not just another characteristic like the capacity for language or higher mathematics. . . . If a being suffers, there can be no moral justification for refusing to take that suffering into consideration. No matter what the nature of the being, the principle of equality requires that the suffering be counted equally with the like suffering—insofar as rough comparisons can be made—of any other being.[7]

Singer draws from this the radical conclusion that, since animals other than humans also experience pain and pleasure, their pains and pleasures must be counted in the utilitarian calculus.

This view is of tremendous importance to the project of this book. For, while many animals, such as dogs or monkeys or even rats, can experience pain and pleasure, it is not the case that the very earliest of human beings can. So, in their very early stages, human embryos have no moral status in Singer's view, and may be used and experimented upon at will.

At the same time, Singer recognizes that sapient beings that have an achieved capacity for reason and self-awareness have lives of greater worth than beings that have not achieved such a capacity. So, human beings who have achieved not just sentience but self-consciousness and the immediately exercisable capacity for moral reflection are considered "persons" and of greater value than merely sentient animals. But human beings do not achieve *this* status until quite late—certainly not until sometime after birth. So while late fetuses and even very young children have some moral claim, because they have interests and can experience pain and pleasure, they can be sacrificed for the sake of science or medicine or even family needs if the interests of developed human persons can thereby be best satisfied.

And this brings us to what is perhaps the most crucial point concerning all forms of utilitarianism and consequentialism: within any such ethic, there will always be human beings who are dispensable, who must be sacrificed for the greater good. Utilitarianism fails to respect, in a radical way, the dignity and rights of individual human beings. For it treats the greater good, a mere aggregate of all the interests or pleasures or preferences of individuals, as the good of supreme worth and value, and demands that nothing stand in the way of its pursuit. The utilitarian thus cannot believe, except as a convenient fiction, in human rights, or in actions that may never be done to people, regardless of the consequences.

We see such thinking, sadly, in much of the moral reflection that goes on concerning human beings at the beginning of their lives. Such reflection is often dominated entirely by concern for the great good that some say can be obtained by research on human embryos, whether left over from IVF or produced, perhaps by cloning. Sometimes the further Benthamite claim is made that embryonic human beings have no moral standing because they cannot feel pain and pleasure, and thus have no interests. But if we abandon this faulty view of value, it is clear that human beings can have interests even when they do not and cannot experience pain and pleasure. If a human embryo is a human being, then its life is a part of it, and it—indeed, he or she—the human embryo, is benefited when it keeps its life, and is harmed when that life is taken away. Similarly, a comatose person, who, let us assume, can feel no pain, does not thereby lose his interest in being treated with dignity by his family. Surely we would think that he was made worse off if others used him for sexual purposes, even though he would never know about it.

Utilitarianism and consequentialism have played a critical role in disposing many people toward treating human embryos as mere material for scientific research. But these are deeply flawed theories: as we have shown, they either rely upon a false theory of value, or they attempt to weigh, commensurate, and maximize where it is impossible to do so. They certainly should be rejected as the basis for distinguishing the just from the unjust treatment of human beings at any developmental stage.

KANT AND DEONTOLOGY

The so-called deontology of Immanuel Kant would seem a more promising place to begin one's ethical reflections. Kant articulated what he regarded as the master principle of morality in three different formulations, all of which he believed amounted to the same thing. This claim to identity of meaning seems wrong, as we can see if we look at Kant's two most important formulations. The first is, "Act only in accordance with that maxim through which you can at the same time will that it become a universal law."[8] This formula states an important moral point: we should not, in deciding what to do, act in a way that we would object to in someone else. Someone who, in cutting the cake and taking a piece, takes a much bigger piece than he would want others to take violates this principle (in a relatively trivial case, of course). The immediate maxim, or principle, that he seems to act on is "Take the biggest piece of cake for yourself." But he could not sensibly allow this to be the principle that everyone should act on; he could not, that is, allow it to be a universal moral law. Similarly, Kant argues, one could not willfully break promises, or lie to others to benefit oneself, and will that such maxims be followed by everyone.

This principle is undoubtedly important in our consideration of embryo ethics, and some philosophers have used it to justify restrictions on abortion as well. For how could we will that embryo killing or abortion be permissible in some particular case when we ourselves were once embryos and fetuses? Nevertheless, Kant's principle seems to articulate only one part of ethics, the requirement of fairness. Moreover, philosophers have argued that in the absence of some other, more foundational guiding principle, Kant's principle of the universal law could be accepted and used to generate silly and even fanatical consequences. A radical racist or Nazi might really be willing to suffer discrimination if it should turn out that he had black or Jewish ancestors.

A second Kantian formulation of the first principle of morality seems to cut deeper than this. The formula is: "So act that you use humanity, whether in your own person or in the person of any other, always at the same time as an end, never merely as a means."[9] Despite Kant's claim, this does not seem identical in meaning to the formula of the universal law; rather, it seems especially focused upon the value of human beings, insofar as that value rules out or demands certain forms of treatment.

This principle is most clear in ruling out certain kinds of actions: what does it mean to treat a human being, oneself or another, as a mere means? Certainly, if I believe that your death will be instrumental to my getting the inheritance, to kill you is to treat you as a mere means to my end of getting the money. By contrast, if I ask you for money, and you agree to lend or give it to me, then I have treated you as an end in yourself by letting the decision remain yours—you are the one who determines whether to give or lend the money. I have thus not treated you as merely subordinate to my wishes, like an instrument for obtaining my ends.

This principle too seems to have bearing on the issue of right treatment of human beings at the beginning of their lives. The late Alan Donagan, a Kantian ethicist, for example, holds that this principle generates a further principle that it is impermissible to use force upon another at will. After briefly reviewing the pertinent biological facts, he writes: "Attempts to deny the humanity of zygotes, by declaring that humanity begins at birth, or at viability (that is, at the point when an unborn child, extruded from the womb, could be kept alive) are scientifically obscurantist . . . It follows that the principle *it is impermissible for anybody at will to use force upon another* applies to adult and child alike, to born and unborn."[10]

We believe that Kant's formulation gives voice to an important ethical truth about human beings: they are intrinsically valuable, and are not to be subordinated, as consequentialists allow, to the purposes of others, or the demands of some alleged "greater good." Nevertheless, we believe also that Kant's formula can be improved upon. The notion of treating humanity as an end in itself is, unfortunately, somewhat vague: how is it that the person can be positively respected, and what are the dimensions of the person that we can fail to respect? Further, Kant's ethics put a justifiable emphasis on not violating other persons, but they do not integrate this question into concerns with human flourishing or well-being; indeed, in Kant, such concerns are deliberately kept at arm's length from questions of ethics.

The two objections are related, for we will argue that in fact the nature of the person, and hence the ways in which the person can be benefited and harmed, respected or violated, are made known to us in part through an understanding of the goods that lead to human well-being and fulfillment. So the view that we propose to explore and defend next is, like Kant's, committed to the dignity and rights of human persons, but, unlike Kant's view, it concerns itself with human goods—that is, constituent aspects of the well-being and fulfillment of human beings.

NATURAL LAW
AND HUMAN FULFILLMENT

Natural law theorists hold that the foundations of morality are to be found in the well-being and fulfillment of human persons and the communities they form.[11] But unlike classical utilitarianism, with its monistic account of the good as pleasure, natural law theory understands human fulfillment—the human good—as variegated. There are many irreducible dimensions of human well-being and flourishing.

This is not to deny that human nature is determinate; rather, it is to affirm that our nature, though determinate, is complex. We are animals, but are also rational. We are individuals, but are also social. We both know and transform reality. The multiplicity of human goods that constitute the basic aspects of human well-being reflects this complexity of our nature: we could not be fulfilled if we were attentive to but one dimension of our well-being.

We call the most fundamental dimensions of our well-being "basic human goods." They are goods, obviously, because they are good for us; they fulfill us in the various dimensions of our being. But they are basic because they give reasons for us to act that do not need grounding for their intelligibility and appeal in some further reason. In this respect, the basic goods, which we will identify shortly, are unlike other goods ("instrumental goods") that are pursued only because they help us to attain or achieve something else. So no one takes medicine just for its own sake, or pursues money just in order to have it. Money and medicine are instrumental goods; they are pursued for the sake of something else.

The basic goods, by contrast, are those that can rationally be pursued for their own sake, and which just as such fulfill us in certain respects as human persons. Moreover, such goods perfect and fulfill all human beings. So it is possible to act for the sake of a human good not just for one's own sake, but for the sake of others; and one has good reason to do so, as we shall see, because friendship and living in harmony with others is itself a basic good, an aspect of human well-being.

The basic goods include, we believe, the following. As animate, bodily creatures, our lives and our health are basic goods: we can intelligibly act simply in order to promote or preserve life, in our own person or that of others.

As rational creatures, knowledge is, for us, a good to be pursued for its own sake; human beings are better off knowing than in ignorance (which is not to deny that there are, in certain circumstances, things one is better off not knowing). Of course, knowledge, like all the basic goods, can also be pursued for the sake of something else; but, like life and health, the pursuit of knowledge for its own sake also gives meaning to our actions, a meaning that does not require some further justification. Similarly, human beings can take pleasure in works of art, and pursue aesthetic experience for its own sake.

Human beings not only can know, but can transform their world through action. They do this in work and in play, which, when pursued as forms of excellence of performance, are humanly fulfilling. People can, again, work for the sake of something else; but no one needs a further reason to do good work, or to play well, than the goodness of work and play themselves.

Human beings are fulfilled not only alone, but in community. The goods of community include friendship, the uniting of a man and a woman in marriage, and living in just and peaceful societies. Each of these goods contributes in a constitutive and not merely instrumental way to human well-being, and does so in respects different from any other.

Two further goods complete our list. Each is similar to the goods of community in a way. All those goods require forms of harmony, for the wills of the members of the community, whether that community is a community of two friends, or of husband and wife, or of political equals, must be harmonized with one another. But so must one's will be harmonized, on the one hand, with whatever source or sources of transcendent meaning exist in the universe, and, on the other, with those aspects of one's self that can conflict with one's choices: the deliverances of practical reason, and one's emotions and dispositions. The good of "religion" corresponds to the former sort of harmony, the good of all around "practical reasonableness" (or "authenticity") to the latter.

The nature and multiplicity of these goods brings out again the crucial failing of consequentialism. Each of these goods is fulfilling of human beings in a way that differs from the way of all the others; each offers something that the others do not. Indeed, even each instance of a good offers something that another instance of the same good does not: one who pursues knowledge through philosophy is fulfilled in a way different from one who pursues knowledge through, say, history. The goods and their instantiations, are, as they figure in options for morally significant choice, therefore, *incommensurable*; there is no "greatest good for the greatest number" that provides the standard for right action.

Rather, the standard for right action is to be found in the concept of a proper orientation to all the goods, an orientation that does not arbitrarily favor any good or person, is not hostile or indifferent to any good, and is alive to the demands of the goods that they be pursued for the sake of human well-being. In the most general way, we could describe this attitude as a will open to and compatible with the ideal of integral human fulfillment—the fulfillment of all human persons in all aspects of their well-being and flourishing. But this really is an ideal—it is not a concrete state of affairs to be pursued, as consequentialists suggest.

Thinking about the proper orientation of the will in this way helps us to identify a number of moral norms as binding on human beings: norms such as the Golden Rule, which requires fair treatment of other human beings, rather than an arbitrary favoring of some over others. Similarly, a will compatible with integral human fulfillment would actively seek the goods, and in creative and social ways, rather than remain satisfied by the mere appearances of knowledge, such as could be induced by drugs, or by mindless or repetitious or individualistic ways of pursuing the goods.

We see such norms at work, for example, in responsible science. Responsible scientists really want the truth—their experiments are designed to bring out what is really the case, not just what they want to be the case, or what will please others. They seek new and creative ways of pursuing the truth, but do so in a cooperative venture with other scientists, both those they work closely with, and those who form the broader scientific community. And they seek to benefit all of humanity by pursuing the frontiers of knowledge.

So far, then, it might seem that the sort of scientific and technical work with which we are most concerned in this book, research on human embryos, is the model of ethically responsible research. For the embryo researcher certainly seems to seek the truth with others, and for the benefit of humanity.[12] Yet this would be too hasty a conclusion.

Consider two further norms. If a morally upright will is one of openness to the ways in which the basic goods direct us toward the well-being and fulfillment of all human persons, then it is surely morally wrong to damage or destroy any instance of a basic human good out of hostility or anger. And in our common-sense moral reflections, we often think of this as the norm that governs the most obvious and frequent sorts of moral wrongs: we grow angry at someone and speak hurtful words, or destroy their possessions, or, in the worst cases, injure or kill them.

But perhaps just as frequently, we believe, moral wrongdoing occurs not because of negative feelings, but because of positive benefits to be achieved, or desires to be satisfied, precisely by engaging in acts that damage certain instances of basic human goods. For example, people occasionally lie out of spite or malice, but people perhaps lie even more often in order to achieve benefits for themselves or others whose welfare they care about, or to avoid serious harm. A will compatible with integral human fulfillment rules out this kind of damage or destruction of a basic human good just as much as it does damage or destruction that flows from hostility to goods or persons.

So consider the following cases: perhaps a scientist could successfully find a cure for cancer if he could only perform lethal experiments on some cancer patients (perhaps patients who will die soon anyway). Or suppose that a dying wife's suffering could be spared if only her husband could administer a lethal mix of drugs to her. Or suppose a student's academic career could be rescued if only his pregnant girlfriend would have an abortion to rid them of the unborn child she carries. In each case, good ends are pursued through means that involve deliberate damage or destruction of instances of a basic human good—in each of these cases, the good of human life itself.

It follows that a norm forbidding killing is not a norm that applies only when an agent is motivated by hostility, hatred, or anger. Killing is impermissible also when it is motivated by the best of intentions, for even though the end might be good, when killing is the chosen means, even if chosen reluctantly, the will is opposed to integral human fulfillment.[13]

HUMAN RIGHTS

What we have said so far will help us to cast some light on disputed questions about human rights and human dignity. This discussion will, in turn, lead to our final claims in this chapter about our responsibilities to the very youngest members of the human community.

Human rights exist if it is the case that there are principles of practical reason that direct us to act or refrain from acting in certain ways out of respect for the well-being and dignity of the human being whose legitimate interests may be affected by what we do. We have just shown that there are such principles, and have identified some of the most important of them. Such principles emerge from the necessity of willing in a way compatible with integral human fulfillment, and from the awareness of the basic human goods as the constitutive elements of such fulfillment.

But there are differences between the principles. Some, such as the principles requiring creative and cooperative action in pursuit of human goods, are affirmative and quite open-ended. Decision is required on the part of agents about how to pursue, when to pursue, and what goods to pursue. Because there are many human goods, and many ways of pursuing them, it is not possible to say in advance for some particular agent, or for all agents, how that, or those, agents should work creatively and cooperatively in pursuit of goods such as life and knowledge. Agents must take account of their circumstances, relations to others, and even personal preferences. Someone who has a hard time concentrating in school is unlikely to do well by choosing, say, a career in philosophy.

Now it is possible to speak of rights in regard to such principles. For example, if Mr. Smith has made a commitment to help Ms. Jones in respect of her scientific research, Jones might be said to have a right to Smith's help. But she does not seem to have a general right to such help from just anybody. Similarly, there is a general duty to help those in great need if an agent can provide such help without disproportionate inconvenience. Perhaps the one who can help is an individual, perhaps a group, perhaps a state; when speaking of a right to some aid—education, health care, and so on—we need to ask: Who is supposed to provide the education or health care, and to whom? Why should those persons or institutions be the providers? And, in considering in particular the role of the state, what place should the provision of education or health care occupy on the list of social and political priorities? Is it better for education and health care to be provided by governments or by private providers?

To some extent, these questions even go beyond the application of moral principles. They require prudential judgment in light of the contingent circumstances people face in a given society. Often, there is not a single, uniquely correct answer. And the rights identified at the end of deliberation might be rights that apply only in some circumstances or at certain times. We should hesitate to call such rights absolute, or inviolable, or universal.

But other moral principles are different. By identifying a type of action as one that always involves damage or destruction to a basic human good, we can identify an action type as being always incompatible with a will to integral human fulfillment. And if this type of action would therefore be always and everywhere wrong for anyone, then we can speak of a corresponding absolute and inviolable right.

Thus, one basic human right that almost all natural law thinkers, including the authors of this book, would say is of this absolute and inviolable sort is the right of an innocent human person not to be directly killed or maimed. It is this right that is violated when someone makes the death or injury of another person the precise object of his action. It is the right that grounds the norm against targeting noncombatants in war, and that grounds the norms against abortion, euthanasia, the killing (or even taking) of hostages, and so on. In such cases an absolute moral principle is violated, and in the violation, human beings are intentionally harmed and their human rights are violated. Rights of this sort are thus radically unlike the sorts of rights we looked at earlier. They are the foundation of the rightful treatment of all human beings.

HUMAN DIGNITY

We often speak of human dignity as being protected by human rights, and of its being violated when those rights are violated. So we should say how the notion of human dignity ties into the discussion so far.

It seems to us that the natural human capacities for reason and freedom are fundamental to the dignity of human beings— the dignity that is protected by human rights. The basic goods of human nature are the goods of a rational creature, a creature who, unless impaired or prevented from doing so, naturally develops capacities for deliberation, judgment, and choice. These capacities are godlike (in a limited way, of course). In fact, from a theological vantage point, we could say that they constitute a certain sharing—again, in a limited but real way—of divine power. This seems to be what is meant by the otherwise extraordinarily puzzling biblical teaching that man is made in the very image and likeness of God.[14]

Still, whether or not one recognizes biblical authority, or believes in a personal God, it is true that human beings possess a power traditionally ascribed to divinity—namely, the power to be an uncaused causing. This is the power to envisage a possible state of affairs, to grasp the value of bringing it into being, and then to act by choice, and not merely impulse or instinct, to bring it into being. That state of affairs may be anything from a work of art to a marriage. Its moral and cultural significance may be great or comparatively minor. What matters is that it is the fruit of deliberation, judgment, and choice.

Human dignity, then, is clearly related in at least two ways to the basic goods and to human rights. On the one hand, it is the basic goods that constitute the reasons for which we freely choose: it is thus because we are oriented to the goods as reasons for action, and are not, as the other animals are, motivated by mere instinct, that we are creatures with dignity, and the subjects of rights. On other hand, it is with respect to the basic human goods as instantiated in our lives that our dignity can be either respected or violated. For, since the basic goods are constitutive aspects of our human nature and well-being, to serve and honor the goods is to serve and honor us, and to damage or destroy the goods is likewise to damage or destroy us. By respecting and promoting the basic goods of human beings, we serve the cause of human rights; by damaging the basic goods of persons, we violate their human rights.

And here we see the connection between the findings of this chapter and those of chapters two and three. For we noted in chapter three that many philosophers have been struck, as are we, by the apparently transcendent features of the human being—the capacities for reason and freedom. Such philosophers have wanted to call beings of this sort "persons," to mark them off from the rest of the (subpersonal) world of nonhuman animals and nonliving things. Persons, those philosophers further claim, as do we, are the subjects of rights, and the objects of moral duties and responsibilities. Philosophers working in a Kantian vein would say, for example, that it is always wrong to treat a person as a mere means, rather than as an end in him- or herself, a being with worth and dignity, rather than just a thing.

With all these claims we agree. But the philosophers discussed in chapter three were alike in thinking that the person was something other than the living human animal that we see when we look in the mirror. This has a variety of unfortunate consequences in ethics. For if we are not, by nature, bodily beings, then clearly bodily human life cannot be a basic good of persons.

There would be, at any rate, no absolute and inviolable right to life in any such view. And similar consequences abound with respect to the other basic goods.

But even more damaging than its repugnant moral conclusions is the simple falsity of metaphysical dualism: neither the readers nor the authors of this book are nonbodily persons inhabiting nonpersonal bodies, as our arguments in chapter three showed. We are rational animal organisms of the human species—human beings. And we have from the very beginning of our lives—from the embryonic stage—been thus.

But we showed also that it is human beings who have the capacities identified as personal—the capacities for reason and free choice. These capacities belong to us by our nature, by virtue of being human creatures. So we—human beings, not human souls or human minds—are persons. And this has significant consequences for morality, just as does the denial of this claim by metaphysical self-body dualists.

For, by the earlier argument, if we are persons, then as bodily beings we have human dignity. And that dignity is served or disrespected by our attitude, and the attitudes of others, toward the basic human goods, including the good of human life. So our dignity is violated when the basic goods are deliberately damaged or destroyed in our person, as when someone intentionally takes another human being's life. That action, as an assault on human life, is an assault on human dignity no matter the victim's age or size or stage of development. We become subjects of human dignity, in other words, from the point at which we begin to exist as human beings, and we are, for the same reasons, the subjects of absolute human rights from precisely that point as well.

But we showed in chapter two that in the vast majority of

cases, excluding only cases of monozygotic twinning, human beings come to be by the completion of fertilization, when there is a single-celled zygotic member of the human species able to direct its own integral organic functioning and development toward maturity. It follows that at that point there exists a subject of human dignity and human rights, and that any choice to deliberately damage or destroy such a subject is a violation of an inviolable right, the human right to life.

And this, surely, is what goes on in the vast majority of cases of embryonic experimentation: early human embryos are dismembered and destroyed in order to produce stem cells, or in order to investigate the features of embryonic development. In this, embryonic human beings and their lives are treated just as means; their lives are held cheap, to be spent in an effort to serve other ends. But no matter how noble those ends, to pursue them in this way is fundamentally wrong. It is an injustice.

CONCLUSION

What we have said to this point in this book generates some strong claims, but claims we think we have shown to be eminently defensible. The crucial claims are these: First, (most) human beings begin at fertilization, and successful human fertilization always produces a human being (even if something will later cause twinning). Second, we, the authors and readers of this book, and all others essentially like us are human beings. Third, human beings as such are the subjects of rights, including the absolute right not to be intentionally killed. Thus, fourth, lethal research on human beings from their earliest, i.e., zygotic and later embryonic, stages is morally wrong and a violation of human rights.

In a more perfect world, perhaps the debate could end here. However, there will be those unconvinced by the arguments mustered so far, and to these interlocutors we address the following three chapters.

In the next chapter we will return to the issue of self-body dualism, but this time from a slightly different perspective. For not all who use the language of "personhood" in order to exclude embryonic human beings from moral consideration are metaphysical dualists. Rather, some would be happy to say that they, and all like them, are human beings who began as zygotes or embryos, yet they would deny that all human beings are worthy of respect. "Personhood" in this view is a status that human beings attain, or that is bestowed on them socially. We shall argue, in chapter five, that this view is deeply misguided.

In chapter six and the beginning of chapter seven, we address a challenge to a different part of our argument, the conclusions drawn in chapter two. There we argued that all human beings (except at least one of pairs of monozygotic twins) begin at fertilization (even clones begin at this point, though fertilization means something slightly different in this case). Yet there are currently philosophers who argue that until the possibility of twinning is over, there is no individual human being. Others claim that the early embryo does not in some other way possess the unity of a single organism. We will show that these claims are unwarranted. We will also argue against a number of other challenges to our view, such as the assertion that human embryos are only "potential human beings," and the claim that cloned human embryos are not human beings (or even embryos) at all.

In the second part of chapter seven, we address some final challenges to our moral conclusions. Specifically, we look at claims that the imminent death of so-called "spare" embryos justifies using them in biomedical research from which some good might come. Then we will examine arguments that attempt to show that lethal experimentation on human embryos does not involve intentional killing.

By the end of this book we hope to have shown definitively that human embryos, whatever their origins (i.e., whether the product of natural conception or cloning or some other process of embryogenesis) and whatever their otherwise intended destination (i.e., whether created for implantation, experimentation, or left in cryopreserved storage) are rational animal organisms of the human species, and hence persons whose dignity demands full moral respect.

CHAPTER 5

Moral Dualism

. . . . . .

The authors and readers of this book and all other human individuals are not nonbodily beings who "have" or "inhabit" or "supervene on" animal bodies. Human beings *are* animals. We are members of a certain animal species—Homo sapiens. Any whole living member of that species is a human being. His or her nature is a *human* nature. Such a nature is a *rational* nature. Human beings are *rational animals*. Now, a human (rational) nature is not something a human being *acquires* at some point after he or she comes into existence, or can lose prior to ceasing to exist. Of course, embryonic, fetal, and infant human beings must develop themselves to the point at which the basic natural capacity for characteristically human (rational) mental activity is fully actualized in the form of immediately (albeit intermittently) exercisable capacities for conceptual thinking and practical deliberation and choosing. But the basic natural capacity is inherent in human nature. So we have it from the point at which we come into existence. And when is that? Most of us (probably including some monozygotic twins) came into existence as whole living members of the human species at fertilization as single-celled zygotes. This is the earliest stage in embryonic development, and, as such, the earliest stage in the life of a human being. Some monozygotic twins (perhaps all, though probably not) came into existence by a process not involving fertilization—a process occurring after fertilization producing a single- or multicelled embryo.

Do these facts settle the debate over the moral status of embryonic human beings? No, for some philosophers who concede that human embryos are human beings deny that all human beings have dignity or a right to life. They say that *persons* have these qualities but insist that not all human beings are persons. All human beings begin life as nonpersons, and some (i.e., the cognitively impaired) never become persons. And any human being may (by becoming severely cognitively impaired) cease being a person prior to ceasing to exist.

Consider, for example, the set of attitudes manifested by the philosopher David Boonin toward his son, Eli. Boonin writes, in his *A Defense of Abortion*, that on his desk are several pictures of his son at various ages. But "through all the remarkable changes that these pictures preserve, he remains unmistakably the same little boy." Boonin then goes on to say:

> In the top drawer of my desk I keep another picture of
> Eli. This picture was taken on September 7, 1993, 24
> weeks before he was born. . . . There is no doubt in my
> mind that this picture, too, shows the same little boy at a
> very early stage in his physical development. And there is
> no question that the position I defend in this book entails

that it would have been morally permissible to end his life at this point.[1]

We commend Boonin for his candor. But we think that his position mires him in a terrible moral mistake; indeed, we will argue that it is a variation of a mistake with which all of us are familiar, and that most of us try to avoid: the mistake of supposing that some human beings are inferior to others on the basis of accidental characteristics. When it is a matter of race or ethnicity, color or gender, origin or outlook, our culture resolutely and rightly holds that what matters is the fact of humanity, and not any other property shared by some but not others. But, by the same token, in considering the status of embryonic humans, what should matter is the fact of their humanity. They should not be regarded as inferior to other members of the human family based on age, size, location, stage of development, or condition of dependency.

In this chapter, we examine efforts to justify positions much like Boonin's. We first look at the claim that personhood is a result of the development of certain properties or abilities. In this view, humans become persons when we have achieved the relevant properties or capacities. There are many varieties of this view, depending upon which properties and capacities a philosopher thinks are necessary for personhood. We look, in particular, at an influential argument advanced by Judith Jarvis Thomson; by refuting her general thesis, we hope to show that the whole family of developmental arguments is flawed.

We then look at the view that holds that personhood is not developed but bestowed: human beings become persons when others decide to regard them as persons. We discuss two representatives of this view, Ronald Green and Carson Strong, and argue that this position too is misguided. Finally, we look at three further arguments that are used to suggest that a human being is not as such the subject of human rights. The first argument points to an alleged symmetry between human beings at developmental stages prior to the formation of the brain and brain-dead human bodies. The second suggests that embryos cannot have rights because people do not typically grieve for them at their deaths. And the third proposes to infer from the high rate of embryo loss in early stages of pregnancy that embryos cannot really be persons. All three arguments, we show, fail to cast reasonable doubt on the case we have made over the previous chapters: that each human being, from the beginning of his or her existence, possesses inherent human dignity and should be accorded full moral respect.

THE DEVELOPMENTAL VIEW

The developmental view of personhood denies that human beings at early developmental stages are persons.[2] But unlike the position criticized in chapter three, the developmental view grants that human beings come into being at fertilization (or slightly later). It contends, however, that humans become bearers of rights only much later, when, for example, we develop the proximate or immediately exercisable capacity for self-consciousness, or for language, and so on. Those who advance this argument thus concede that each of us who is now an adult was once a human embryo, and they do not identify the self with a nonphysical phenomenon, such as consciousness.

They do claim, though, that being a person is an accidental attribute. It is accidental in the way that someone's being a musician or a basketball player is an accidental attribute: as we argued in chapter three, one can come to be a musician or basketball player, and cease to be one as well, without ceasing to be the kind of being one is *essentially*. So while metaphysical dualists disagree with us in regard to an ontological issue—the issue of *what* we are—moral dualists differ with us, and with the prolife position generally, in regard to the moral question of *when* a human being is owed moral respect.

Judith Jarvis Thomson has argued for this position—in a way that can be stated without reference to any particular putative marker of personhood—by comparing the right to life with the right to vote. Thomson argues that "[I]f children are allowed to develop normally they will have a right to vote; that does not show that they now have the right to vote."[3] So, according to this position, it is true that we once were embryos or fetuses, but in the embryonic and fetal stages of our lives, we were not yet valuable in the special way that would qualify us as having a right to life. We acquired that special kind of value and the right to life that comes with it only at some later point in our existence.

We can begin to see the error in this view by considering Thomson's comparison of the right to life with the right to vote. For Thomson fails to note the fact that some rights vary with respect to place, circumstances, maturity, ability, and other factors, while other rights do not. We recognize, for example, that one's right to life, or one's right not to be enslaved, does not vary from place to place, as does one's right to vote or to drive. One of the authors of this book, RPG, has the right to vote in New Jersey, but not in South Carolina. The other, CT, has that right in South Carolina, but not in New Jersey. And neither has the right to vote in Great Britain. But regardless of where or when they travel, both RPG and CT have the right to life—and they do not lose it when they visit each other or travel abroad.

Some rights, in other words, accrue to individuals only at certain times, or in certain places and situations, while others do not. But to have the right to life is to have moral status at all; to have the right to life, in other words, is to be the sort of entity that can have rights or entitlements to begin with. And it is to be expected that this right would differ in some fundamental ways from other rights, such as the right to vote.

In particular, it is reasonable to suppose (and we give reasons for this in the next few paragraphs) that having moral status at all, as opposed to having the right to perform a specific action in a specific situation, follows from an entity's being the kind of thing it is. And so, just as one's right to life does not come and go with one's location or situation, so it does not accrue to someone by virtue of an acquired property, capacity, skill, or disposition. Rather, this right belongs to a human being at all times that he or she exists, not just during certain stages of his or her existence, or in certain circumstances, or by virtue of additional, accidental properties.

Our position is that we human beings have the special kind of value that makes us subjects of rights by virtue of what (i.e., the kind of entity) we are. The defenders of the developmental view believe we are valuable by virtue of some ability we have come to have. But as we saw in chapter three, there are obvious difficulties with requiring human beings to be capable of actually exercising this ability (whatever it is) right now. The proponents of the developmental view do not wish, for example, to exclude from the status of "persons" human beings who are asleep or who are in reversible comas. So the additional attribute will have to be a capacity or potentiality of some sort. They will wish to say that sleeping or reversibly comatose human beings *are* persons because they have the potentiality or capacity for higher mental functions.

But as we have argued in chapter three, human embryos and fetuses also possess, albeit in radical form, a capacity or potentiality for such mental functions; human beings possess this radical capacity by virtue of the *kind* of entity they are, and possess it by coming into being as that kind of entity. Human embryos and fetuses cannot, of course, immediately exercise these capacities. But because they are human beings—not dogs, cats, or squirrels—they will, if not prevented by extrinsic causes, in due course and by intrinsic self-direction, develop to the point at which they are able to immediately exercise these inherent capacities. Such development is natural to what early human beings already are.

It is crucial to distinguish two sorts of capacities for higher mental functions that a substantial entity might possess. First, such a being might possess an immediately (or nearly immediately) exercisable capacity to engage in such a function. RPG has the immediately exercisable capacity to speak French, and CT has the nearly immediately exercisable capacity to do so—but unlike RPG he needs to brush up a bit. But second, there is a basic, natural capacity to develop oneself to the point where one does perform such actions. Both CT and RPG have had this capacity since they came into being; but no dog, cat, or squirrel has ever or will ever have this capacity. Similarly, both RPG and CT have and always have had the radical capacity to speak Finnish;

the fact that neither has this as a proximate capacity should not cause anyone to doubt this claim.

But is it reasonable for defenders of the developmental view of personhood to require the first sort of potentiality, which is accidental, and not the second as the basis for moral respect? It is not; there are three decisive reasons against supposing that the first sort of potentiality is required to qualify an entity as a bearer of the right to life.

First, the developing human being does not reach a level of maturity at which he or she performs a type of mental act that other animals such as dogs and cats do not perform until at least several months after birth. A six-week-old baby lacks the immediately or even nearly immediately exercisable capacity to perform characteristically human mental functions. So, if full moral respect were due only to those who possess a nearly immediately exercisable capacity for characteristically human mental functions, it would follow that six-week-old infants do not deserve full moral respect. If abortion were morally acceptable on the grounds that the human embryo or fetus lacks such a capacity for characteristically human mental functions, then one would be logically committed to the view that, subject to parental approval, human infants could be disposed of as well.[4]

Second, the difference between these two types of capacities is merely a difference between stages along a continuum. The proximate or nearly immediately exercisable capacity for mental functions is only the development of an underlying potentiality that the human being possesses simply by virtue of being the kind of entity he or she is. The capacities for reasoning, deliberating, and making choices are gradually developed, or brought toward maturation, through gestation, childhood, adolescence, and so on. But the difference between a being that deserves full moral respect and a being that does not (and can therefore legitimately be disposed of as a means of benefiting others) cannot consist only in the fact that, while both have some feature, one has more of it than the other.

In other words, a mere quantitative difference (having more or less of the same feature, such as the development of a basic natural capacity) cannot by itself be a justificatory basis for treating different entities in radically different ways. Between the ovum and the approaching thousands of sperm, on the one hand, and the embryonic human being, on the other, there is a clear difference in kind, as we showed in chapter two. But between the embryonic human being and that same human being at any later stage of its maturation, there is only a difference of degree.

Thus, when a human being comes to be, a substantial entity that is identical to the entity that will later reason, make free choices, and so on, begins to exist. So those who propose an accidental characteristic as qualifying an entity as a bearer of the right to life (or as a "person" or a being with "moral worth") are ignoring a radical difference among groups of beings—the radical difference between sperm and egg on the one hand, and the human being on the other—and instead focusing on a mere quantitative difference as the basis for treating different groups in radically different ways.

A racist picks out shade of skin as a more important characteristic than common humanity in deciding the worth of human beings. Now, between human beings and all other nonhuman animals, there is a radical difference in kind: human beings, unlike every other animal species, have the basic natural capacity for reason and freedom. But between any two human beings, the difference in color will always be only a difference of degree, a difference that makes no difference to the sorts of beings that each is. The racist is thus behaving radically unfairly toward those he regards as inferior by picking out a characteristic that should be irrelevant to moral respect. We hold that prejudice and discrimination against human beings at early developmental stages commits a species of the same error (though it is easier to see how the error can be made by persons of goodwill).

There is a third and related problem with the developmental view. The acquired qualities that could be proposed as criteria of personhood come in varying and continuous degrees. There are, in fact, an infinite number of degrees of the development of the basic natural capacities for self-consciousness, intelligence, or rationality. So if human beings are worthy of full moral respect (as subjects of rights) only because of such qualities, and not by virtue of the kind of being they are, then, since such qualities come in varying degrees, no account could be given of why basic rights are not possessed by human beings in varying degrees. The proposition that all human beings are created equal would be relegated to the status of a myth—a noble (or, perhaps, not-so-noble) lie.

For example, if developed self-consciousness were the grounds of human dignity, then because some people are more self-conscious than others (that is, have developed that capacity to a greater extent than others), some people would be greater in dignity than others, and the rights of the superiors would trump those of the inferiors where the interests of the superiors could be advanced at the cost of the inferiors. This conclusion would follow no matter which of the acquired qualities generally proposed as qualifying some human beings (or human beings at some stages) for full respect were selected.

Clearly, developed self-consciousness—or desires or the ability to use language and so on—are arbitrarily selected degrees of development of capacities that all human beings possess in (at least) radical form from the coming into existence of the human being until his or her death. So it cannot be the case that some human beings and not others possess the special kind of value that qualifies an entity as having a basic right to life, by virtue of a certain degree of development. Rather, human beings possess that kind of value, and therefore that right, by virtue of *what* they are; and all human beings, not just some, and certainly not just those who have advanced sufficiently along the developmental path as to be able immediately (or almost immediately) to exercise their capacities for characteristically human mental functions, possess that kind of value and that right.

It is worthwhile to point out a possible misunderstanding of our argument here. Michael Sandel has suggested in a recent book that this type of argument is a version of a "sorites paradox." In a classic sorites argument, it is held that there is no difference between a grain of sand and a heap, because it is impossible to specify, in a nonarbitrary way, a particular number of grains that make a heap. Similarly, Sandel claims that arguments about personhood such as ours work by suggesting that there is no moral difference between a child and a blastocyst, since it is impossible to specify, in a nonarbitrary way, where that moral difference lies. But, says Sandel, "The fact that there is no nonarbitrary point where the addition of one more grain will bring a heap does not mean that there is no difference between a grain and a heap."[5] Similarly, the "fact of developmental continuity from blastocyst to implanted embryo to newborn child does not establish that a baby and a blastocyst are, morally speaking, one and the same."[6]

What the sorites analysis overlooks, however, is that we *have* specified a nonarbitrary difference in human development. For while it is true that there is no nonarbitrary difference between a blastocyst and a later embryo or infant, there *is* a nonarbitrary difference—a difference in kind—between male and female gametes and the single-celled human embryo. The embryo is *a new human being*—the same complete human organism, as Sandel himself seems to acknowledge, as the later child and adult. While subsequent changes exist on a continuum, the change from gametes to a new human individual does not. The union of gametes effects a substantial change that brings into being a new and distinct entity. The changes from embryo to fetus to infant to adolescent to adult are merely changes in degree of natural development of the entity—in this case a human individual, *a human being*—in question.

Since human beings are intrinsically valuable and deserving of full moral respect by virtue of *what* they are, it follows that they are intrinsically valuable from the point at which they come into being. As we have shown, even in the embryonic stage of our lives, each of us was a human being. Each of us was, therefore, from the earliest stage of embryonic development onward worthy of moral concern, respect, and protection. Contrary to Sandel's assertions, there is nothing arbitrary or unreasoned here. And contrary to Boonin's assertions, it would have been morally wrong for him or anyone else to have deliberately killed his son Eli at the beginning of his life.

THE ATTRIBUTION VIEW
OF PERSONHOOD

Consider the following difficulty for the defender of the developmental view, surveying the work of the various philosophers who promote it. Jones, for example, believes that personhood arises when there exist the biological precursors to the brain. But Roberts, another defender of the developmental view, believes that personhood begins with the development of consciousness and the ability to experience pain. And Brown, a third defender of the position, holds yet a different view: personhood arises when a being is first self-conscious and capable of some thought, however primitive.

These three views are considerably different from one another, and have radically different implications for ethics. The first view would make human beings the subjects of moral rights from a relatively early period of prenatal development. The third view would see rights and moral worth as arising only sometime after birth. Yet what can possibly ground a nonarbitrary argument for one of these markers rather than the other?

This was the thrust of our argument in the previous section: attributes such as those defended by Jones, Roberts, and Brown are matters of degree, and, considered as actual attributes, rather than considered as radical potentialities, they are accidental to a being's nature; a human being is just as much a human being before he or she can experience pain (for example) as after.

The arbitrary nature of such determinations might, therefore, lead our would-be defender of the developmental view to embrace a somewhat different account of personhood, one that makes explicit what seems implicit in the developmental view, as already discussed. He might, that is, come to hold that what makes a human being worthy of moral respect, and a subject of moral rights, is a *decision* by some other individual or group of individuals that this human being will henceforth be accorded moral respect and be a subject of moral rights. We will call this position the Attribution View, for according to its proponents, personhood comes about for human beings because it is attributed to those human beings.

The bioethicist Ronald Green is someone who holds and defends the Attribution View. Green was an ethicist on a panel formed by the National Institutes of Health in 1994 at President Clinton's request to address the moral questions surrounding embryonic creation and research. That panel recommended that research be permitted on so-called spare embryos left over from IVF procedures, and allowed the creation of embryos for some research purposes. Green agreed with the first decision, and recommended an even more permissive approach than the second. Green describes his reasoning on these matters in his book, *The Human Embryo Research Debates.*

Green's view on moral attribution seems to follow from a more general and even more radical thesis about the nature of knowledge and reality—in particular, biological reality. Green holds that biology involves continuous processes, rather than definite events. Thus, biological science and understanding is not a "matter of discovering important events in the entity that must dictate our judgment."[7] We cannot even say with respect to the coming into being of the human organism that it took place at such and such a time or stage, or was completed by such and such a time or stage. Rather, in order to determine when a particular event, such as the beginning of the human organism, has taken place (and thus, when a particular human being began to exist), we must make a decision.

But on the basis of what sorts of criteria are we to decide? Decisions are, after all, guided by values. Thus, Green writes: "[I]dentifying these events requires us to identify and apply the values that underlie our thinking. Drawing on these values, we must decide which events are most important to us among the range of alternatives."[8]

It is worth mentioning, before turning to Green's views about moral status, just what a radical view this is about the nature of biological reality and scientific knowledge. For example, if the identification of biological events is a matter of decision, and not fact, then there is nothing in principle to prevent two people, or two groups, from holding radically different but equally valid positions about when something had happened. Of course, sometimes different scientists disagree sharply about the truth of some scientific claim. But our ordinary assumption is that when two scientists do disagree, at least one of them must be wrong. It is impossible, in other words, for two scientists, or groups of scientists, to hold contradictory positions and both be right.

But any view that holds, in regard to some type of claim or other, that there are no facts, no "right answers," but that answers, knowledge, or truth are merely a matter of decision, radically removes the possibility of error by making virtually every answer a right one. And this, in turn, radically eliminates, it seems to us, any possible motivation for studying biology or any other area of science. For we study biology or chemistry or physics in order to find out what the world is like independently of what we have said about it, or wish were the case about it, or think might be true about it. When we study the natural sciences—indeed, when we study in any area, including humanistic disciplines such as philosophy, theology, or history—we study with a view to discovering the truth. And if truth is merely a matter of what we decide, what is in accord with our "values," then there is not much point in study after all.

So Green's account of science is very problematic. But it is no more problematic than his views on moral status. Green himself criticizes some of the views that we have criticized already. For example, he argues against the extreme views of Michael Tooley and Peter Singer that allow infanticide, and which also give to many nonhuman animals the moral status of human beings. And he argues against those who, like the authors of this book, think that embryos merit full moral respect. But Green locates in all the views he criticizes a core, and common, mistake:

> All these problems stem from the failure to realize that judgments of "humanity," "personhood," or any similar determination of moral protected-ness are not a matter of definition, of finding the intrinsic biological property of an entity that makes it morally protectable, but are instead the outcome of complex moral choice involving many competing considerations. Sometimes these considerations have less to do with the nature of the entity than with the implications of a boundary marker itself.[9]

Green's view on the matter of moral status is thus the same as his view about biological events: there is no "fact of the matter" about whether a human being is worthy of moral respect or not; there is only the need for decisions to be made in accordance with our "values."

If moral status is to be determined on the basis of our choices, and our choices are to be guided by our values, then it is natural to ask what sorts of values should guide our choices in respect to human embryos. In describing the NIH panel's deliberations, Green writes that the panel asked itself, "How much were we prepared to limit researchers' activities? How much were we willing to put the health of children and adults at risk?"[10] And he is quite clear that he thinks the most important values here are not values like the "sanctity of life," but rather values such as reproductive freedom, medical advances, and scientific progress. From the standpoint of these values, to decide that very early embryos are human persons, worthy of full moral respect, would be a disaster.

Thus, Green rightly describes his approach as pluralistic and pragmatic—it involves no moral absolutes or even relatively stable principles, but rather a general appeal to the costs and benefits that "we" would think most important in considering embryo research.

Green's pluralistic pragmatism is interestingly different from the position of another supporter of the Attribution View, Carson Strong. Like Green, Strong believes that moral worth is something bestowed upon human beings, rather than a status grounded in the nature of those beings. But unlike Green, Strong advocates a consequentialist approach to the problem of bestowing moral status.

In Strong's approach, we need to find the "model" or paradigm case of a human being with rights, and identify which characteristics of that being are such that we think them morally relevant to their special status. We then measure other human lives against the model to determine whether or not they are sufficiently similar to also possess moral worth. But what guides this determination of closeness is a concern for the consequences: "Are they similar enough to make reasonable the claim that failure to confer a right to life upon them would result in adverse consequences" for other, model human beings?[11]

So, for example, while infants are in some obvious respects far away from the model, it would be potentially dangerous to treat them as having no moral worth, even though Strong does not really think they do have moral worth. Strong thinks we should "confer" moral "standing" on infants, despite what he takes to be the moral fact that they are not persons, and even grant them a "right to life" for what are essentially extrinsic reasons:

> [Infants] are viable, sentient, have the potential to become self-conscious, have been born, and are similar in appearance to the paradigm of human persons. Although some of these characteristics have been put forward as a sufficient condition for normative personhood of fetuses or infants, none of them by itself constitutes compelling grounds for personhood. What is often overlooked is the significance that should be given to the aggregate of these characteristics. The combination of these similarities, I would maintain, is significant enough to warrant conferring upon infants serious moral standing, including a right to life.[12]

The similarities are important, because by failing to treat infants as having a right to life, we might weaken our respect for the lives of the model human beings. But as we get farther away from infants, and closer to the beginnings of life, the differences between younger human beings and model adults increase, and the similarities decrease:

> As the dissimilarities increase, there remains a possibility of adverse consequences, but the likelihood and magnitude of such consequences diminishes. As these diminish, the amount of weight that should be given to these consequentialist considerations decreases. This amounts to saying that the degree of conferred moral standing that the individuals should have decreases.[13]

Finally, when we get to embryos and "preembryos"—that is, embryos at a stage in which twinning is still possible, "conferring a minor degree of moral status" is all that is reasonable, because of their great dissimilarity from the model human person.

Does the Attribution View mark a philosophical or moral improvement over the Developmental View? We argued earlier in this chapter that one of the biggest philosophical difficulties with the Developmental View was its deep-rooted arbitrariness. Rather than make moral status a question of the nature of a being, the Developmental View established as criteria characteristics that were vague, or existed only on a continuum, or were accidental, or all three. Such philosophical difficulties amounted to a moral problem: to base moral respect on such characteristics, rather than on a being's essential nature, is unfair—it focuses on what is arbitrary, rather than on what really matters.

But both the arbitrariness and the unfairness are only exacerbated in the case of the Attribution View. Consider the problem of arbitrariness first.

We argued that the right to life, unlike the right to vote, does not vary from place to place or time to time for the same entity. This is because the right to life is in a strong and obvious sense the foundational right for persons. It is the right on which all other rights are predicated, and marks whether a being is a being of moral standing at all. If the right to life depended upon, for example, a particular and exercisable ability, then some human beings would possess that right earlier than others, and some would never possess it.

But if moral standing is a result of a decision, and is bestowed upon a human being by others, then the same human beings might both have the right to life and not have the right to life at the same time and in the same place. What, for example, would be the case if a mother conferred a right to life upon her unborn embryo and a father did not? Or if one large part of a population conferred the right to life upon human embryos, while another large part of the population did not? Like Green's views about the nature of biological facts, this view about the rights of human persons is absurd, for it results in an obvious contradiction.

But, of course, in fact, it is unlikely that Green, or Strong, would think in terms of competing judgments of moral status. And this is because, in fact, to the extent that decisions about status are made and have consequences, they are typically made by those with enough power to be able to impose their decisions upon others. Thus, where the scientific establishment and the powers of the state collude to make research upon embryonic human beings legally permissible, both Green and Strong would, in all likelihood, speak of the decision that "we" have come to as if that decision reflected a truly social choice. They would fail to note that, by their own theories, as long as there are those who recognize the right to life of the early embryo, then the early embryo will still have that right, even at the same time as it does not have that right.

Nevertheless, the difficulty the previous paragraph points to will stand. Even though the theory of bestowed personhood is philosophically deficient, a culture that takes it as its starting point for moral deliberations will think that a proper decision has been made when the group in power decides that some other group does not have the right to life. And this is why the Attribution View is so deeply morally flawed. In practice, the Attribution View amounts to an apology for the decisions of those in power to treat as nonpersons those without power and without adequate social support to provide protection.

We conclude, then, that both the Developmental View and the Attribution View fail to provide convincing reasons against our central moral thesis in this book: that each human being throughout his or her life has inherent human dignity and is the subject of moral rights and deserving of moral respect. Both views are arbitrary in their assessment of which human beings should be considered persons; neither is a sound basis on which to make moral decisions about the moral status of human beings.

Now, some people will still try to resist the force of this conclusion, and will argue that, contrary to what we have shown, there are good reasons for treating embryonic human beings differently than human beings at later developmental stages. We now turn to such arguments.

BRAIN DEATH

Michael Gazzaniga, a member of the President's Council on Bioethics, has suggested that the human person comes into being only with the development of a brain. Prior to that point, we have a human organism, but one lacking the dignity and rights of a person. Human beings in their earliest stages of development may therefore legitimately be treated as we would treat organs available for transplantation (assuming, as with transplantation, that proper consent is given for their use, e.g., by parents). In developing his case, Dr. Gazzaniga observes that modern medicine treats the death of the brain as the death of the person, authorizing the harvesting of organs from the remains of the person, even if some physical systems are still functioning and can be mechanically maintained for a time. But if a human being is no longer a person with rights once the brain has irreversibly ceased functioning, then surely a human being is not yet a person prior to the development of the brain.

This argument suffers, however, from a damning defect. Under prevailing law and medical practice, the rationale for "brain death" is not that a brain-dead body is a living human organism but no longer a person. Rather, brain death is accepted because the irreversible collapse of the brain destroys the capacity for self-directed integral organic functioning of human beings who have matured to the stage at which the brain performs the key role in integrating the organism. What is left is no longer a unitary organism at all.

By contrast, although an embryo has not yet developed a brain, its capacity to do so is inherent and developing, just as the capacity of an infant to develop its brain sufficiently for it to actually think is inherent and developing. Moreover, the embryo is clearly exercising self-directed integral organic functioning, and so is a unitary organism; and, because of the kind and orientation of this functioning, it is clearly a human organism.

Unlike a corpse—which is merely the remains of what was once a human organism but is now dead, even if particular systems may be mechanically sustained—a human being in the embryonic stage of development is a complete, unified, self-integrating human organism. It is not dead, but very much alive. A factor or factors other than the brain makes possible its self-integration and organic functioning. Thus it is that we, and other defenders of early human life, insist against so many who misstate the case that the embryo is not a "potential life" but is rather a "life with potential."

The embryo is a potential adult in the same way that fetuses, infants, children, and adolescents are potential adults. It has the potentiality for agency, just as fetuses, infants, and small children do. But, like human beings in the fetal, infant, child, and adolescent stages, human beings in the embryonic stage are already, and not merely potentially, human beings. All these various stages are developmental stages of a determinate and enduring being who comes into existence as a single-celled human organism and develops, if all goes well, into adulthood by a gradual and gapless process over many years. There is thus no symmetry between a human embryo—a living human being with its life ahead of it—and a brain-dead corpse, whose life is over.

GRIEF

A different argument suggests that since people frequently do not grieve, or do not grieve intensely, for the loss of an embryo early in pregnancy, as they do for the loss of a fetus late in pregnancy, or a newborn, we are warranted in concluding that the early embryo is not a human "person" worthy of moral respect.

The absence of grieving is sometimes a result of ignorance about the facts of embryogenesis and intrauterine development. Consider the importance the phenomenon of quickening has had historically. Although it does not mark any change in the nature of the infant in the womb, quickening is, for the mother, the time from which she can feel the baby moving about. Given the relevant embryological facts, it is clearly irrelevant as a marker for personhood. Nevertheless, if people are told, as they still are in some places, that there simply is no human being until quickening, then they are likely not to grieve, or not grieve as intensely, at an early miscarriage. But people who are better informed, and women in particular, very often do grieve even when a miscarriage occurs very early in pregnancy.

Granted, some people informed about many of the embryological facts are nevertheless indifferent to early miscarriages. But this is often due to a reductionist view according to which embryonic human beings are misdescribed as mere "clumps of cells," or "masses of tissue," and so on. Further, some people who recognize that the embryo is a human being believe for philosophical reasons of the sort we have criticized that the embryo is nonetheless not a person. The emotional attitude one has toward early miscarriage is typically and for the most part an effect of what one thinks—rightly or wrongly—about the humanity or personhood of the embryo. Hence, it is circular reasoning to use the indifference of people who deny that human beings in the embryonic stage deserve full moral respect as an argument for not according such respect.

Moreover, the fact that people typically grieve less in the case of a miscarriage than they do in the case of an infant's death is partly explained by the simple facts that they do not see the baby, hold the child in their arms, talk to him or her, and so on. The process of emotional bonding is typically completed after the child is born—sometimes, and in some cultures, not until months after the child is born. This is particularly true in situations in which infant mortality is high; parents sometimes will not bond strongly with children when the risk is great that they will lose them soon.

However, a child's right not to be killed plainly does not depend on whether the child's parents or anyone else has formed an emotional bond with him or her. Every year—perhaps every day—people die for whom others do not grieve. This does not mean that they lacked the status of human beings who were worthy of full moral respect. It is thus simply a mistake to conclude from the fact that people do not grieve, or that they grieve less, at early miscarriage that the embryo has less dignity or worth than human beings at later stages of development.

NATURAL EMBRYO LOSS

Now let us turn to yet another argument advanced by those who favor research involving the destruction of human embryos. Some people conclude that embryonic human beings are not worthy of full moral respect because a high percentage of em-

bryos formed in natural pregnancies fail to implant or sponta-
neously abort. This inference, we believe, is fallacious.

It is worth noting, as standard embryology textbooks point
out, that a number of these unsuccessful pregnancies are actually
due to severe chromosomal defects.[14] It seems plausible to infer
that in some cases, these defects are so significant that a human
embryo probably failed to form. As a result, what is lost in many
cases may not be a human embryo. For example, a defect in fertilization resulting from the penetration of an empty ovum (lacking its nucleus and thus its DNA) by two or more sperm may give
rise, not to an embryo, but to a complete hydatidiform mole. To
be a complete human organism (human being) an entity must
possess a developmental program (including both its DNA and
epigenetic factors) oriented toward developing a brain and nervous system; that is, it must, by virtue of its biological makeup,
possess, at least in root form, capacities for characteristically human mental activities, even if disease or defect should at some
point impede the further actualization of those capacities.

Of course, through some chromosomal defect, a genuine
human being might be prevented from developing to maximum
functioning; the fact that there is a defect in preventing the actualization of the program, and even a defect in the program itself,
does not mean that they do not have the program at all.[15] In such
cases, the entity is a human being, albeit a handicapped one. But
if fertilization is radically defective, then what will be produced
is not an organism with the active capacity for self-directed development as a whole living human being, but rather a disordered growth. And a percentage of unsuccessful pregnancies
involve growths of this sort, rather than true embryos.

A second point concerns the nature of the argument itself,

which rests upon a variant of the naturalistic fallacy. It supposes that what happens in "nature," i.e., with predictable frequency in the absence of human intervention, must be morally acceptable when deliberately caused by human action. Since embryonic death in early miscarriages happens with predictable frequency, the argument goes, we are warranted in concluding that the deliberate destruction of human beings in the embryonic stage is morally acceptable.

The unsoundness of such reasoning can easily be brought into focus by considering the fact that historically the infant mortality rate has been very high. (Sadly, there are some places where it is high even today.) If the reasoning under review here were sound, it would show that human infants in such circumstances could not be full human beings possessing a basic right not to be killed for the benefit of others. But that, of course, is certainly wrong. The argument is thus a failure.

WHOM TO RESCUE?

At a meeting of the President's Council on Bioethics, Michael Sandel posed an interesting question and developed a line of argument meant to show that our view about the status of the human embryo has implications that almost no one would be willing to accept.[16] Suppose that a building is on fire, and Jones, who is trying to escape the building, can save a crate of ten frozen embryos or one five-year-old girl, but not both. By saving a crate of embryos, Jones would, by our account, be saving many human beings; and yet it seems plausible that most reasonable agents, among whom we will include Jones, would save the five-year-old girl. Can we agree that this choice is reasonable, given our view of the nature of frozen embryos as human beings, equal in fundamental worth and dignity to human beings at later developmental stages? After all, Jones has, by our account, the opportunity to save ten human beings, yet he saves only one. Does our willingness to accept Jones's choice as morally legitimate show that, in truth, we do not regard human embryos as we regard children at later stages of development, namely, as full members of the human family?

We agree that considering the case just as described by Professor Sandel, most people in Jones's circumstances would choose to rescue the girl. However, we do not believe that this shows that human embryos are not human beings, or that they may be deliberately killed in order to produce stem cells.

The first thing to notice is that the case as described is not, in fact, analogous to the suggestion that we should perform embryo-destructive research for the benefits we might provide to, say, five-year-old children. For in that case, we are invited to *kill* human embryos for the sake of harvesting parts of their bodies for use in experiments to benefit others. But in the fire case, there is no killing: the death of the embryos who are lost when Jones opts to save the girl is not intentional killing, but the sort of death we accept as a side effect in various cases of conflict, limited resources, or triage.

Second, there are differences between the embryos and the five-year-old girl that are or can be morally relevant to the decision concerning whom to rescue. For example, the five-year-old will suffer great terror and pain in the fire, but the embryos will not. Moreover, the family of the five-year-old presumably loves her and has developed bonds of attachment and affection with her that will mean much greater grief in the event of her death than in the event of the death of the embryos. While these concerns would not justify killing, they can play a legitimate role in determining how we may allocate scarce resources, and, in some cases, whom we should rescue. Thus, it is morally relevant in some cases where choices of whom to rescue must be made that a person whom we could save is (for example) our own son or daughter, even if saving him or her means that we cannot save, say, three of our neighbors' children.

Third, there could be circumstances in which people could agree that it would be reasonable for a particular person to save the embryos, even if other people, including people with no personal attachment to either the embryos or the girl, might be drawn to rescue the girl. For example, if Jones happens to be the mother or father or grandparent of the embryos, Jones might well choose to rescue them, and most people would not regard this as immoral. (By contrast, everyone would agree that it would be immoral even for a parent or grandparent to kill someone else's child in order to harvest, say, a heart or liver needed to save the life of a child or grandchild.)

The possibility that resources might be used, and even, perhaps, lives risked to save the frozen embryos might call to mind the story with which we began this book, of Noah and his dramatic rescue from the floods of Katrina. That narrative shows, we believe, that the choice to rescue embryos is not necessarily fanciful or unreasonable. And there is another point worth considering, which the story of Noah brought to light. Suppose that someone, whether connected to the embryos or not, chose to save them despite the fact that it meant forgoing the opportunity to save the girl. Suppose further that the embryos were soon thereafter implanted and taken by their gestational mothers to birth, and then grew to adulthood. If, upon reaching their twenty-first birthdays, the ten young adults organized an event to honor and thank the person who had rescued them when they were embryos, could the rescuer in good faith accept their praise and gratitude for rescuing *them*? Clearly the answer, as with Noah, is, "Of course." But had Jones "rescued" only a crate of sperm or oocytes, he could not claim that he had rescued any children, but only elements that could be later used to produce children.

The problem with Sandel's argument becomes still more evident if we consider some other cases. For example, imagine a fire from which Jones must choose to rescue either four pregnant women or six men. Many people would likely choose to rescue the pregnant women, precisely because they would reasonably judge that they were rescuing eight human beings rather than six.

Finally, imagine that Jones is faced with the choice of rescuing three comatose patients or a five-year-old girl. Many people who disagree with us about embryos agree with us that comatose persons are human beings entitled to full moral respect. Yet no doubt many of these same people would opt to save the girl, rather than the three individuals in comas. Does that mean that they would consider it legitimate, in a different case, to kill one or more of the comatose individuals to harvest vital organs needed to save the five-year-old girl? Not at all. Choices about whom to save are subject to the particular facts of the situation without requiring a comparative valuing (or devaluing) of lives. But choices to kill are always devaluing choices. When such distinctions are adequately made, we can see that Sandel's objection does not threaten our position.

A CONCLUDING POINT

We have shown, we believe, that all attempts to claim that an embryonic human being is not worthy of moral respect are fatally flawed. But it is worth noting that through all the argumentation of this book we have not found it necessary or even helpful to make claims about the human soul.

It is sometimes said that opposition to human embryo killing is based upon a controversial theology of "ensoulment." However, none of what we have had to say has anything to do with a religious doctrine of ensoulment, or with whether an embryo who dies will have spiritual remains in the form of an immaterial soul. That is an interesting theological question, but one that is unnecessary to the moral debate and to questions of public policy.

It is further worth pointing out that even the Catholic Church does not try to draw scientific inferences about the humanity or distinctness of the human embryo from theological propositions about ensoulment. In fact, the Catholic Church works the other way around. Someone who wanted to talk the pope into declaring something that the Church has never up to this point declared, namely, that the human embryo is "ensouled," would have to prove his point by marshaling (among other things) the scientific facts. The theological conclusion would be drawn on the basis of (among other things) the findings of science about the self-integration, distinctness, unity, determinateness, etc., of the developing embryo. So things work exactly the opposite of the way some advocates of embryo-destructive research, who think they know what the Catholic Church says about ensoulment, imagine they work.

The straightforward consequence of this point is this: the arguments of this book do not rely on any premise, claim, or authoritative teaching of any form of revealed religion. These arguments are not in any way sectarian or religious. They, are, rather, arguments using what the late John Rawls called "our common human reason"—a power, it is worth reiterating, that adult human beings exercise by virtue of having developed to the point of immediate exercisability an inherent natural capacity they possessed in radical form from the very beginning of their lives simply by virtue of being human beings.

Chapter 6

New Objections
to the Humanity of the
Early Embryo

*   *   *   *   *   *   *

In chapter two we provided biological evidence, taken from the standard embryological textbooks, to show that there can be little question concerning *what* the early embryo is. The early human embryo is a human being at the earliest stage of his or her development. Not a "potential" human being, or a "pre" human being, or a mass of cells, or mere tissue, but an individual member of the species Homo sapiens. This claim has been central to all the subsequent argumentation of this book. We have argued that we, the readers and authors of this book, and all others substantially like us, are essentially human beings. And we have argued that human beings as such are persons worthy of fundamental moral respect, and subjects of fundamental human rights.

Despite what we take to be clear and convincing biological evidence, however, there have been a number of attempts in recent years to deny the claim that human embryos are human beings. The reasons for such denials are various, ranging from differing interpretations of biological fact to philosophical theses about what it means to be an individual. In this chapter and the next, we address a number of these claims, showing, claim by claim and argument by argument, that the best account of what the human embryo is remains the account given in chapter two.

Two of the most important arguments in this recent literature about the humanity of the embryo can, we think, be treated together. Both concern the question of whether the early human embryo is an individual (we will shortly explain why this is an important question). One argument denies that the embryo is an individual, and hence a human being, on the basis of a consideration of whether the life of an embryo at the earliest stages is sufficiently unified; the other denies individuality and humanity because of the possibility, mentioned at various points in this book so far, of monozygotic twinning. We believe that both arguments require, essentially, the same sort of response, so we first describe each view, and then argue against them together.

We then turn to a more diverse set of claims and arguments, some philosophical, some popular. Beginning with the popular, we refute the surprisingly common claim, sometimes merely implied, that early embryos are not human because they do not look human. We then look, in succession, at arguments by Ronald Bailey, a science writer for *Reason* magazine, and Lee Silver, a professor of biology at Princeton University. Bailey argues that embryos are no more persons than are the vast number of somatic cells that make up an adult human's body; Silver argues that the early embryo does not have the type of life characteristic of a human being, but only a form of "vegetative" life. In response, we demonstrate the misunderstandings and misinterpretations on which these arguments rest.

In chapter seven, we address arguments from two members of the President's Council on Bioethics. Michael Sandel, a political theorist at Harvard University, has argued that just as acorns are not oak trees, neither are embryos human beings. And Paul McHugh, a professor of psychiatry at Johns Hopkins University, has acknowledged the humanity of human embryos conceived through the fusion of male and female gametes, but denied that embryos brought into being through human cloning are, properly, human beings.

Throughout our discussion of these arguments, we must keep in mind, and at times reiterate, much of what has already been argued in this book. For it seems reasonable to infer that, if embryos are not human beings and are not individual organisms, then the case for performing lethal experimentation upon such embryos is quite strong, assuming that the potential benefits approximate what proponents of embryo-destructive research claim. But, given the arguments of chapter five, we are confident that if our claim that human embryos are human beings holds up, then there is no reasonable case for lethal experimentation on human embryos, for if these embryos are human beings, they are also persons; and all persons are due a level of respect that is simply inconsistent with treating them as disposable research material.

INDIVIDUALS, ORGANISMS, AND PERSONS

The first two arguments we address share a significant feature in common: each denies that the early human embryo can be considered an individual, a single whole being of a particular kind.

Why is this denial considered so crucial? The answer is easy to understand. It belongs to our paradigmatic understanding both of what it means to be an organism of a particular species, and of what it means to be a person, that both organisms and persons are *wholes*, entities sufficiently unified that they can reasonably be considered to be one particular being. In short, organisms and persons are individuals.

Consider, for example, the difference between the cat Tibbles and the bag of bottles you have collected to bring for recycling. Tibbles is a genuine individual, a whole being, who exists as a complete entity, with his own life and fairly distinct boundaries that separate him from everything else in the world. If we were counting how many individuals were in the room, we would count Tibbles himself as one of them. But we would not count Tibbles's parts—his organs, his cells—as independently existing individuals, for they are all "caught up in" Tibbles's life.[1] But if one of Tibbles's parts were to be removed—if we were to amputate a leg of Tibbles's, then, because it would no longer be part of Tibbles, it would constitute a new entity in the room.

The bag of bottles is not like Tibbles, however, in several ways. For it seems that the bag of bottles is merely a collection of things (the bottles), kept together with an artificial boundary (the bag). The bag of bottles does not form some one thing; it is not a unified integrated whole, except in a very loose sense. If we were counting individuals in a room, we might count the bag with the bottles; but we might equally count each of the bottles. For when we take the bottles out of the bag, it does not seem that many new individuals have come to be, but only that we have disaggregated what was previously together *only* as an aggregate, not as a unity. The various bottles do not together constitute a single entity, and in this way, they are unlike the parts of Tibbles, which are just that—*parts* of a *whole* cat.

Now consider the following passage from the philosopher Peter van Inwagen about the cells that compose the early human embryo after its first mitotic division:

> They adhere to each other, but we have seen that that is no reason to suppose that two objects compose anything. The zygote was a single, unified organism, the vast assemblage of metabolic processes that were its life having been directed by the activity of nucleic acid in its nucleus. No such statement can be made about the two-cell embryo. No event, I should say, is its life. The space it occupies is merely an arena in which two lives, hardly interacting, take place. . . . [2]

As is obvious, van Inwagen believes the cells of the early human embryo to be more like the bottles in the bag than like Tibbles: they are not parts of a unified whole, but a mere aggregate of cells that only adhere to one another. Similarly, philosophers Barry Smith and Berit Brogaard write that the cells of the early embryo "form a mere mass, being kept together spatially only by the thin membrane (the *zona pellucida*), which is inherited from the egg-cell before fertilization, but there is no causal interaction between the cells."[3] So Smith and Brogaard too see the cells as analogous to our bag of bottles, but not to our cat Tibbles.

If van Inwagen, Smith, Brogaard, and others are correct, however, and the early human embryo is not an individual, but a mere collection, then it is not a human being, for human beings are individual organisms of the species Homo sapiens. And if it is neither a human being nor an individual, then it is certainly not a person; it would therefore plausibly not be due the same fundamental form of respect due to full members of the species.

This is the first line of argument directed at the individuality of the embryo, and hence its humanity. Its central claim is that the early human embryo is insufficiently unified to count as one whole individual. The second argument is likewise directed against the individuality of the early embryo. But this time the key premise concerns the biological possibility of monozygotic twinning.

The phenomenon of twinning is still not perfectly understood. But it is clear enough that in the early stages of embryonic life—possibly up to as late as the fourteenth day prior to beginning of gastrulation—an embryo may divide into two distinct organisms, each with the potential to develop to maturity. The process has been replicated at very early stages in test tubes: the embryo can be pulled apart, its cells being separated, and the separated cells will seemingly readjust so as to develop themselves into multicellular human organisms. It is unclear whether, in nature, a similar external disturbance is necessary to pull apart the early embryo, or whether there is some genetic tendency toward division.

Why should this capacity be troubling? Proponents of the argument from twinning against the humanity of the embryo assert that the potential for division indicates that the embryo does not, while it still can so divide, possess the intrinsic unity characteristic of a whole distinct organism. Something potentially two, in other words, cannot really be one. So the suggestion is that as long as twinning is still possible, what exists is not yet a unitary human being, but only a mass of cells, each one at first totipotent, then pluripotent, but each allegedly independent of the others.

It is this alleged independence that we believe is the real issue. For this is a question of biology: Does the biological evidence indicate a mass of merely adhering cells, or a unified entity? This biological question must be distinguished from a conceptual question about individuals: Can something that is genuinely one entity split so as to become two? Or must any entity that can do this be something other than one to begin with?

This conceptual question of whether an entity that is genuinely one could be split so as to become two has a ready answer. Consider the parallel case of division of a flatworm. Parts of a flatworm have the potential to become a whole flatworm when isolated from the present whole of which they are a part. Yet no one would suggest that prior to the division of a flatworm to produce two whole flatworms, the original flatworm was not a unitary individual.

Likewise, at the early stages of human embryonic development, before specialization by the cells has progressed very far, the cells or groups of cells can become whole organisms if they are divided and have an appropriate environment after the division. But that fact does not in the least indicate that prior to such an extrinsic division the embryo is other than a unitary, self-integrating, actively developing human organism. It certainly does not show that the embryo is a mere clump of cells.

THE UNITY OF
THE EARLY HUMAN EMBRYO

With the conceptual question clarified, let us return to the biological question. Is the early embryo operating in a way characteristic of a single whole organism? In assessing the status of the embryo, we need to answer three questions. First, does the embryo act like a whole organism? Second, are the parts differentiated in any way, such that they seem to play the different functional roles in a whole characteristic of the parts of a multicelled organism? And third, is there a relationship between the parts themselves, such that the behavior of some parts is coordinated with the behavior of others, possibly through communication mechanisms, or are the parts really only a loose aggregation of cells with little connection to one another?

We should note first that the embryo in its first week seems to have three "goals." In describing these goals, and how the embryo pursues them, we find the answers to all three of our questions: we see the embryo acting as a unified, integrated whole. We see the different functional roles of those parts. And we see that the parts are themselves internally related, and not just externally tied together.

The first goal is to get itself to the uterus, where it can implant; as we have seen, this is something that the embryo plainly does as a unified whole. The second is to develop the structures necessary to make implantation possible, such as the embryoblast and trophoblast. This too is a process carried out by the embryo, and is fairly complex. For example, the trophoblast itself differentiates into the cytotrophoblast and the synctiotrophoblast. The latter plays an important role in implantation, eroding endometrial tissues to enable the embryo to burrow, and eroding maternal blood vessels, thereby enabling "the primordial utero-placental circulation" of blood.[4]

The embryo's third goal appears to be to preserve its structural unity against various threats. Thus, the zona pellucida protects the embryo from polyspermy (fertilization by multiple sperm) and from premature implantation. In serving these tasks, the zona seems like the real, albeit temporary, external boundary of the developing embryo, rather than a mere container for an otherwise independent set of cells.

All these goals are further subordinated to a larger goal of this early organism, the goal toward which implantation is directed: to receive adequate nourishment in a congenial environment, so as to be able to continue its growth and development. So the early embryo has many of the obvious goals of a whole organism, and undertakes directed activity in service of those goals.

Moreover, earlier stages of the embryo's activity are clearly oriented toward doing what is necessary to make later stages possible. Consider, for example, the process of compaction, occurring on day two or three. At the two-cell stage, the embryo begins synthesizing a glycoprotein called E-cadherin or uvomorulin, which will be instrumental in the compaction process at the eight-cell stage, the process in which the blastomeres (the individual cells of the embryo at the blastocyst stage) join together, flattening and developing an inside-outside polarity.[5] This seems to be further evidence that the embryo acts as a unified, integrated whole, directing its own growth and development from within. And we should note again that Moore and Persaud write of compaction that it "permits greater cell-to-cell interaction."[6]

Even those who deny the individuality of the early embryo have a hard time writing in ways that preserve the sense of their characteristic thesis. Consider the following passage from Smith and Brogaard:

> The blastocyst, on completing its journey along the fallopian tube into the uterine cavity, moves into a position where it is in contact with the uterine wall, to which it adheres via its sticky exterior. Cells on its outer surface then begin to grow rapidly in such a way as to disrupt the surface of the wall. These cells actively burrow into the deeper tissue until they have become completely embedded.[7]

What, we must ask, is the *subject* of this sort of activity? Is it the activity of a unified substance, or is it the activity of a collection of substances? We see here a single self-directed entity, the nature of whose self-direction is species-specific: the course of events outlined by Smith, Brogaard, and others is the characteristic course of activity of the early human embryo in much the same way that it is characteristic of the adult dog to chase rabbits. What is the alternative? Only that the hundreds, and eventually thousands, of cells that are present prior to and during gastrulation and neurulation each has its own species-specific nature that causes them to bring about, each individually, a massively complex state of affairs that has not been coordinated by a single agent.

Do the various cells of the early embryo (once it has begun cleavage) have distinct characteristics and tasks? If not—if they are just a homogenous group of more or less identical cells doing more or less the same thing—we might be led to think that the early embryo is a mere aggregate of those cells, rather than a unified organism. But embryologist Bruce Carlson suggests a far more adequate picture:

> Even at the early stage the blastomeres of a cleaving embryo are not homogeneous. Simple staining methods reveal pronounced differences among cells in human embryos as early as the seven-cell stage. Autoradiographic studies have shown that all blastomeres of four-cell human embryos have low levels of extranucleolar and nonnucleolar RNA synthesis. By the eight-cell stage, some blastomeres have very high levels of RNA synthesis, but other blastomeres still show the pattern seen in blastomeres of the four-cell embryo. Morphological studies show corresponding differences between transcriptionally active and inactive blastomeres.[8]

And clearly, by the time of implantation, the embryo has become internally differentiated enough that it is possible to identify and distinguish the precursor cells of the placenta from the embryo proper.

Moreover, even this relatively late division (relative, that is, to the first week of development) of labor seems to have been determined at earlier stages, and to require the sort of internal coordination of information among the cells characteristic of a multicellular organism. Patrick Lee, summarizing recent studies on mouse embryos, writes that "the sperm entry point into the oocyte influences how the zygote will divide, and which cell (even at the two-cell stage) will give rise to the embryoblast (the embryo proper) or the trophoblast (the chorion and the embryonic portion of the placenta)."[9]

Such early differentiation of cell tasks suggests not only that each cell has its own job but that there is coordination of tasks among the cells; otherwise, it would have to be a mere accident that the several cells enclosed within the zona "happened" to have different, complementary tasks. But the appearance of coordination and indeed communication among cells is strengthened by a general feature of the embryonic system, its regulative nature. Carlson describes regulation as "the ability of an embryo or organ primordium to produce a normal structure if parts have been removed or added. At the cellular level, it means that the fates of cells in a regulative system are not irretrievably fixed and that the cells can still respond to environmental cues."[10]

Carlson gives examples of several experiments that have been performed on early embryos that involve removing cells or adding cells from other sources. Cells may be removed from one very early embryo and integrated into the life of another, even to the point of creating interspecies chimera, such as a goat-sheep. Mouse blastomeres from different embryos can be aggregated together to form a single large embryo. And, perhaps most striking in light of the evidence of cell destination cited by Lee, cells destined to become part of the trophoblast can be moved into the inner cell mass and be integrated into the embryo, while cells from the inner cell mass can be moved to the trophoblast and integrated into placental development. Carlson summarizes:

> Experiments of this type demonstrate that the developmental potential or potency (the types of cells that a pre-

cursor cell can form) of many cells is greater than their normal developmental fate (the types of cells that a precursor cell normally forms).[11]

But these experiments also demonstrate something else: a capacity of the cells to shift their development *in response to the needs of the whole and the tasks of its surrounding cells.* In this respect, the parts of the early embryo operate much as the organs of an adult human being, which have some capacity to compensate for deficiencies in other organs.

The evidence suggests, then, that at the end of the first week, the same organism that came into being at fertilization has continued to grow and pursue its important biological goals. It does this by means of an increasingly differentiated division of labor among the cells, but a division whose original plan dates back to the very act of fertilization. And it pursues its goals, and adjusts for difficulties, by means of communication from cell to cell. It is, it would seem, a single organism, just like a toddler, adolescent, or adult.

However, the clearest evidence that the embryo in the first two weeks is not a mere mass of cells but is a unitary organism is this: if the individual cells within the embryo before twinning were independent of the others, *there would be no reason that each would not regularly develop on its own.* Instead, these allegedly independent, noncommunicating cells regularly function together to develop into a single, more mature member of the human species. This fact shows that interaction is taking place between the cells from the very beginning (even within the *zona pellucida*, before implantation), restraining them from individually developing as whole organisms and directing each of them to function as a relevant part of a single, whole organism that is continuous with the zygote.

Thus, prior to an extrinsic division of the cells of the embryo, these cells together do constitute a single organism. So the fact of twinning does not show that the embryo is a mere incidental mass of cells; and the evidence against this claim likewise serves to refute the first argument, which claimed that the embryo lacked the unity of a single living being. Rather, the evidence clearly indicates that the human embryo, from the zygote stage forward, is a unitary human organism.

Some have argued that integrated development does not in fact occur until at the earliest four days, at compaction, when the individual blastomeres form tight junctions and gap junctions, and the zygotic genome begins to guide development (before which, it is claimed, the maternal mRNA guides at least the first two divisions). In an excellent undergraduate thesis at Princeton University, Evan Graboyes has argued that before this point (the eight-cell stage, at day three or four), the blastomeres are merely physically joined by the zona pellucida but do not act in an internally directed or coordinated manner.[12]

It is true that tight junctions and gap junctions are not formed directly between the cells before the eight-cell stage. But these are not the only types of cellular communication that occur within the blastomeres of multicellular organisms. In particular, there is conclusive evidence of interaction and communication between the blastomeres in the form of differential gene expression from the four-cell stage, and there is good evidence that some differential gene expression occurs even at the two-cell stage.[13]

The first definitive *manifestation* of differentiation into different cell types occurs with the differentiation into inner cell mass and trophoblast (at about day four). Yet distinct changes are occurring in different cells, in particular differential gene expression, to prepare for this specialization. In other words, the phenotypic changes such as differentiation into inner cell mass and trophoblast have already been programmed in the mRNA and embryonic genes that were within the embryo from the beginning, that is, from the point at which a new cell was produced with the union of the sperm and the ovum.

This position is a more reasonable and economical interpretation of the data. The position that the embryo up until day four or even up to day fourteen is only a mass of cells posits a unification or coordination of perhaps over hundreds of cells, occurring with predictable regularity, but without any cause. Between day one and day four, or day fourteen, nothing is added to the embryonic system that could explain the appearance of unity. That is, if the organization or integration is *manifested* at day four, but nothing occurs between day one and day four to account for its production, then that integration was present from day one.[14]

THE EMBRYO
DOES NOT LOOK HUMAN

People who argue that human beings in the embryonic stage do not deserve the level of respect accorded to human beings at more mature stages of development sometimes point out that the five- or six-day-old embryo is very small—smaller than the period at the end of a sentence on a printed page. The embryo looks nothing like what we ordinarily think of as a human being. It has not yet developed a brain, and so does not yet exhibit the human capacity for rationality. Indeed, it has no consciousness or awareness of any sort. It is not even sentient. Could anything seem more unlike the beings that we characteristically think of as persons?

What can be said in reply to these points, beyond what we have already offered? To claims about the size and appearance of the embryo, we must say that it simply begs the question about the humanity (and the rights) of the embryo to say that it does not resemble (in size and shape) human beings in later stages of development. For the five-day embryo looks exactly like what human beings look like at five days old. Each of us looked like that during the embryonic stage of our lives. The *biologically* relevant consideration is not appearance; rather, it is the fact that from the beginning, the embryo possesses the active capacity for self-directed growth and maturation through the various stages of a human life. We all started off small. But that just means that we exist as temporal creatures who grow and mature through time.

Nor, of course, is appearance *morally* relevant. The argument from the appearance of the embryo to the conclusion that it is not a human being is hopelessly weak—it has no scientific credibility. From a moral standpoint, concern with appearance as a marker for moral worth bespeaks an injustice of attitude similar to other noxious forms of prejudice. The "appearance" of the embryo is a mere accident, and has no role to play in reasoned debate about either its nature or moral worth.

ARE EMBRYOS RELEVANTLY LIKE
SOMATIC CELLS?

In defending research involving the destruction of human embryos, Ronald Bailey, a science writer for *Reason* magazine, has developed an analogy between embryos and somatic cells in light of the possibility of human cloning.[15] Bailey claims that every cell in the human body has as much potential for development as any human embryo. Embryos therefore have no greater dignity or higher moral status than ordinary somatic cells.

Bailey observes that each cell in the human body possesses the entire DNA code; each has become specialized (as muscle, skin, etc.) by most of that code being turned off. In cloning, those portions of the code previously deactivated are reactivated. So, Bailey says, quoting Oxford bioethicist Julian Savulescu: "If all our cells could be persons, then we cannot appeal to the fact that an embryo could be a person to justify the special treatment we give it."[16] Since, plainly, we are not prepared to regard all of our cells as human beings, we shouldn't regard embryos as human beings either.

However, Bailey's analogy between somatic cells and human embryos collapses under scrutiny. The somatic cell is something from which, together with other causes, a new organism can be generated. It is certainly not, however, a distinct organism. A human embryo, by contrast, is, as we have argued, a distinct, self-developing, complete, though immature, human organism.

Bailey suggests that the somatic cell and the embryo are on the same level because both have the "potential" to develop into a mature human being. The kind of "potentiality" possessed by somatic cells that might be used in cloning differs profoundly, however, from the potentiality of the embryo. In the case of somatic cells, each has potential only in the sense that something can be done to it so that its constituents (its DNA molecules) can become a distinct whole human organism, that is, a human being, a person.

In the case of the embryo, however, he or she is actively, indeed, dynamically developing himself or herself to the further stages of maturity of the distinct organism—the human being—that he or she already is. The embryo will undergo change; that is, it will be the subject of change. It is not, however, changed into something other than what it is. By contrast, the somatic cell must cease to be that sort of entity—essentially, a part of a whole organism—and be changed into a complete human organism.

True, the whole genetic code is present in each somatic cell. And this code can be used for the guidance of the growth of a new entire organism. But this point does nothing to show that its potentiality is the same as that of a human embryo. When the nucleus of an ovum is removed and a somatic cell is inserted into the remainder of the ovum and given an electric stimulus, this does more than merely place the somatic cell in an environment hospitable to its continuing maturation and development. Rather, it generates a wholly distinct, self-integrating, entirely new entity. In other words, it generates an embryo. And this embryo, which is brought into being by this process, is quite radically different from the constituents that entered into its generation.

Somatic cells, in the context of cloning, then, are analogous not to embryos, but to the gametes whose union results in the generation of a distinct, self-integrating new organism in the case of ordinary sexual reproduction. Sperm cells and ova are not distinct, complete, self-integrating human organisms. As we showed in chapter two, they are, properly speaking, parts of human organisms—parts of the men and women whose gametes they are. Their union can generate a new organism, an entity that is not merely part of another organism. But that organism was never itself a sperm cell or an ovum.

Nor would a person who was brought into being as an embryo by a process of cloning have once been a somatic cell. All adult human beings were once embryos, just as they were once children, and before that infants, and before that fetuses. But none of them—none of us—was ever sperm cells, or ova, or somatic cells. To destroy an ovum or skin cell whose constituents might have been used to generate a new and distinct human organism is not to destroy a new and distinct human organism—for no such organism exists or ever existed. But, if one were to call to mind any particular human being, and imagine that someone might have destroyed that human being during the embryonic stage of his or her existence and development, then it could only have been that particular human being who would have been destroyed.

ARE EMBRYOS RELEVANTLY LIKE STEM CELLS?

Lee Silver presents an argument for the denial of the humanity of the embryo that is, as we shall see, similar in important respects to Bailey's argument. Silver writes, "Embryonic stem cells can develop into an actual person. So, based on the definition of the U.S. National Academy of Sciences, embryonic stem cells are equivalent to embryos. Yet based on the molecular signals that you give the cells, the cells can change from embryonic to nonembryonic and back to embryonic."[17] But the first sentence just quoted is false. Embryonic stem cells are functionally parts of a complete organism; they are not themselves complete organisms.

A human embryo, as we have shown, can, precisely *because* it is a complete human organism, develop to a more mature stage of human development, provided it has an adequate environment and nutrition. The embryo contains an active disposition to develop itself to its next, more mature stage. But this is not true of a stem cell or even a mass of stem cells. Like somatic cells that might be used in cloning, they possess a merely passive capacity to be acted upon in such a way as to contribute functionally to an asexual form of reproduction.

Silver's evidence for his claim that "embryonic stem cells are equivalent to embryos" comes from a discovery within mouse embryology. A mouse embryo can be generated from embryonic mouse stem cells in such a way as to have all of its genetic makeup derive from the initial stem cells. The procedure is somewhat similar to Somatic Cell Nuclear Transfer cloning: an embryonic mouse stem cell is aggregated with a tetraploid mouse embryo. This is an embryo with four sets of chromosomes, rather than the normal two. Such embryos (or embryo-like entities) are severely developmentally defective; they can give rise only to trophoblastic cells (as we saw in chapter two, these are precursors to the placenta and associated tissues), and not to the cells of the embryo proper.

When the embryonic mouse stem cells and the tetraploid embryo are aggregated, a chimeric mouse embryo results in which the cell lineage of the placenta and associated tissues is derived from the tetraploid embryo, and the cells of the mature embryo are derived from the embryonic stem (ES) cells. From this, Silver infers that ES cells can *by themselves* develop into the mature stage of the animal. Since it is often argued that human embryos are human beings because they can "by themselves" develop into mature humans, it follows, according to Silver, that embryos and stem cells are (ontologically and morally) equivalent. But it is absurd to think that ES cells are human beings; so it is also absurd, Silver concludes, to think that human embryos are human beings.

Silver's argument is, as we have noted, similar to Bailey's argument about somatic cells. Both arguments assert that a certain kind of cell—somatic or ES—can become, or can produce by itself, a mature human being, just as a human embryo can. But it is important, and indeed definitive, to note that the phrases *can become* or *can produce by themselves* mean something different when we are talking about embryos than when we are talking about somatic or ES cells.

The crucial point in our argument against Bailey was that the SCNT process *transforms* the somatic cells into entities of a different nature; somatic cells are parts that, treated in the right way, *can become* something other than parts, i.e., they can become complete human organisms. So somatic cells are unlike embryos, which "become" mature human beings in the same way that infants "become" adolescents, i.e., without a change in the kind of entity or being the infant or the embryo is. Somatic cells must become a different sort of entity in order "to become" a human embryo.

But Silver thinks that the production of a mature mouse by the process described above answers this reply: in the process, the more mature organism is derived directly from the ES cells, and so the ES cells do in some sense *by themselves become* whole embryos. Just like embryos, in Silver's view, ES cells also can develop into mature members of their species if they are just given a suitable environment.

In fact, however, Silver just repeats Bailey's mistake. In the case of mouse embryos created by the aggregation of tetraploid embryos and ES cells, the ES cells do not, *by their own internal self-direction,* develop into a mouse. So they are not mouse embryos or their equivalent. The ES cells by themselves can produce mouse embryos in the sense that there is, as it were, a material identity between ES cells and the mouse embryo: the mouse embryo has the same genetic constitution as the ES cells. But this is a bit like saying that a pile of bricks can produce by itself a house—perhaps the house requires no other material for its construction, but it is not the case that the bricks organize themselves and direct the process by which they "become" a house.

But this is exactly what the embryo can and does do. Indeed, this capacity is central to the embryo's nature, as it is not to the nature of an embryonic stem cell. So, just as in SCNT cloning, so here: the manipulation (in this case, the aggregation of the ES cells with the tetraploid embryo) generates a new kind of biological entity. The manipulations involved do much more than merely release an inner capacity of the stem cells. The aggregation of the stem cells with the tetraploid embryo (either by an electric stimulus that erodes the zona pellucida or by injection) does not merely place these cells in an environment hospitable to the process of organic development. Rather, it transforms them from functional parts to component parts of an actively developing whole organism. More precisely expressed: the aggregation of the stem cells with the cells of the tetraploid embryo generates a new organism—an organism that is different in kind from a stem cell.

Silver's argument, like Bailey's, fails because it trades on an ambiguity in the phrase *X produces or develops by itself into Y*. In other words, he is guilty of a fallacy of equivocation. His argument fails to falsify the proposition to which modern embryology attests: that human embryos are complete, though developmentally immature, human individuals—human beings in the embryonic stage of development.

VEGETATIVE
VERSUS SENTIENT LIFE

Lee Silver has articulated a different argument in support of the claim that human embryos are not human beings. Silver says that there are two senses of the term *alive*: a vegetative sense and a sentient sense. He distinguishes what he means by them as follows:

> We now understand vegetative life to mean microbial, animal or plant cells or tissues that exhibit metabolic activity and growth properties, but not the ability to sense and respond quickly to stimuli, or to move rapidly from one place to another. We now understand that sentient life depends upon the existence of higher brain function which allows an animal to respond rapidly to external stimuli.[18]

Professor Silver illustrates this distinction with an example of a man who is shot to death with a bullet to the head. "We can all agree that he is dead, but for at least a short time, nearly all the cells below his neck are very much alive."[19] After the man dies, he continues, the cells and many of the tissues in his body are alive in the "vegetative" sense, but not the "sentient" sense.

With this distinction between vegetative and sentient life (as he interprets it), Silver then argues that if one asks "when life begins," one must give different answers depending upon whether one is asking when "vegetative" life begins or when "sentient" life begins. He writes that if we ask about the beginning of life "in the vegetative sense," the answer is three billion years ago, since "every cell in every human body can be traced back to the first cell that existed."[20] But if we mean sentient life when we ask when life begins, then "since sentience is dependent on higher brain function, it cannot occur in the absence of a functional brain," and "there is no coordinated brain activity in an embryo that is less than eighteen weeks old."[21] So Silver declares that early human embryos have vegetative life, but not sentient life, and therefore they are not human beings:

> If, as I have shown here, newly fertilized embryos (sic)[22] cannot be equated with human beings, then there is no scientific basis for making the claim that 5 to 6 week old embryos—which have no capacity for sentience or any other kind of brain function—are human beings.[23]

At the heart of this argument, however, is a fallacy. Professor Silver confuses the distinction between "sentient life" and "vegetative life" (the life of an animal versus the life of a plant) with the distinction between the life of a whole organism and the life of the tissues and cells that are functionally parts of an organism. When a human being dies from a bullet wound in the head, this is not because the organism has lost its "sentient life" and reverted to "vegetative life." Rather, the organism as a whole—the human being—ceases to function as a unified and self-integrating reality. The organism dies. Cells and many of the tissues, until they decay, now have a distinct life, though no longer as parts of an integrated developing and/or functioning whole. Thus, Silver's argument rests on a confusion of the question. The question is not: When does sentient function (or the immediately exercisable capacity to sense) begin? Rather, the question is: When does the life of this particular human being begin?

This confusion utterly invalidates Silver's argument, for the fact that the early embryo is not sentient (i.e., does not have the immediately exercisable capacity to sense or perceive) provides not the slightest evidence to indicate that this organism is not the same organism (the same living being) as the one that does, at a later developmental stage, sense and, later still, engage in conceptual thought. Nor does it account for the fact that the genetic material, genetic program, and active disposition to develop a functioning brain are already present.

Professor Silver simply ignores the fact that organisms often exist and develop themselves during periods of time in which they lack the immediately exercisable capacities to perform all of the functions typical of their kind. Instead of recognizing that point (that a human being indisputably exists during early developmental stages in which he or she does not yet perform the mental functions toward which he or she is developing), he redescribes the situation as one in which there is first mere "vegetative" life and then later "sentient" life.

The evidence that we presented in chapter two, however—

evidence gathered from the standard scientific works in the field of embryology—shows that this description flies in the face of the established facts. All of the evidence indicates that what occurs is simply the maturation of the selfsame living being so that he or she is eventually able to perform certain acts (sensing, engaging in abstract conceptual thought, etc.) in response to certain stimuli. This development is possible precisely by virtue of the kind of being he or she is—a human being.

After all, it is clear in other species that individuals come to be and live for long periods before they actually perform the acts characteristic of their species. For example, a panther kitten has not yet developed the immediately exercisable capacity to digest meat (an ability that very much determines the cat's whole manner of living); but clearly the panther kitten is a whole member of her species. The same point—but with respect to sensing and conceptual thought—is true of the very young human being. As we pointed out in chapter three, the proper way to identify the nature of an organism is not to look at it merely at one time, but to look at it through time, for it is through time that organisms develop the capacities characteristic of their nature.

Arbitrary distinctions, such as Professor Silver's distinction between vegetative and sentient life, often have problematic but unacknowledged implications. Silver's argument would lead, for example, to the conclusion that anencephalic children are not human beings. And it would imply that the comatose, since they also lack the immediately exercisable capacity for sensing, are not human beings.

In fact, if Silver's argument were correct, it would also follow that a new and distinct organism was generated well after the attainment of sentience when the child acquired the immediately exercisable capacity for abstract conceptual thought, since this human capacity is significantly different and distinct from mere sentience. Mere sentience is, after all, possessed by animals whose killing for food, sport, and other purposes the law freely allows. We should need to distinguish not just between "vegetative" and "sentient" life but also "sapient" life. Silver's logical error dictates this conclusion, but it would be patently absurd to hold that the human being does not come to be until years after birth (when his or her capacity for abstract conceptual thought becomes immediately exercisable).

Moreover, Silver has simply ignored the fundamental question, substituting a different one that is of no relevance to the matter in dispute. All parties agree that a human being is a distinct, whole, living being or organism. What therefore must be squarely faced, as we did in chapter two, is the biological question: When does the life of the distinct whole human being begin? *Whole* or *complete* means neither functionally a part, as are somatic cells, sex cells, or human tissue being preserved in a petri dish, nor a mere disordered growth, such as a tumor or a teratoma. Professor Silver has imported his own meaning of the question into the discussion. He submits a new definition of "human being," and one that is distinctly his own, namely: a human organism that has reached a stage of maturity at which sentient capacities are (or soon will be) immediately exercisable.

But this is not a scientific definition. For this reason, it is difficult to avoid the inference that it has been arbitrarily selected, and given the patina of science, for the purpose of reaching a previously desired conclusion. In his work, Professor Silver seems almost studiously to avoid the question that is really at issue: Is or is not the human embryo the same organism, the same living being, as the fetus, the newborn infant, the child, the adolescent, and the adult it becomes as it matures through the normal developmental stages of a human life?

The embryo is plainly a living being. The child that is born several months later is also a living being. The question Professor Silver must answer, yet avoids, is this: Is that child the same living being? Or is he or she a different one? The leading authorities in human embryology and developmental biology are united in answering this biological question: The child and the embryo are the same living being, the same organism. "Child" and "embryo" merely refer to the same living being at different stages of maturity.

We would ask the following question: Does Professor Silver dissent from this consensus or not? He claims that there is no "sentient" life until week eighteen or later, but he avoids saying whether the living being that is sentient (has the immediately exercisable capacity to sense and perceive) is or is not biologically the same living being as the one that was produced by fertilization, grew by normal cell differentiation, traveled down the uterine tube and implanted on the uterus, and so on.

But there is only one reason to avoid this question, and that is that the answer is so obvious: it is indeed the same living being that engaged in all these activities. So it is only by smuggling into the discussion an irrelevant pseudoscientific definition of "human being," that personal to him, that Silver is able to avoid an undeniable fact of biology.

But doesn't the development of a brain in the embryo mean that there is now something new, some new entity? It does not. In fact, no embryological authority holds that the gradual development of the brain generates a new or separate organism. On the contrary, all hold that the brain emerges in the developing human being on the basis of internal resources and development already programmed into the selfsame living being that begins in the embryonic stage and develops through the natural stages into adulthood. During this growth, all of his or her capacities, such as those for walking, eating, and seeing, as well as those for abstract reasoning, deliberation, and so on, are initially present only in root form. Each only gradually develops with maturation to the point of being immediately exercisable.

Indeed, in human beings, major development of the brain occurs after birth, enabling the child only several months later to develop the immediately exercisable capacity for abstract conceptual thought. Does this mean, as Professor Silver suggests, that the human embryo is not complete, and therefore not a human being? In one sense of *complete*, it is true that the embryo—like the fetus, newborn, and toddler—is not yet complete: it has not yet fully developed the capacities natural to it, and which it already possesses. But this is not the sense of *complete* that we must give in the question: Is the early embryo a complete, whole, distinct individual? In the sense intended by this question, embryos, fetuses, infants, and toddlers are all complete human beings, though immature. They are not mere parts of larger organisms, nor are they disordered growths.

All the distinctions we have made in this discussion are crucial to the debate over early human life. By attending to them, we can see that the only type of reason someone could have for treating the difference between having the immediately exercisable capacity for sensing and not having it as morally significant is a philosophical or theological reason, but not a scientific one. The content of any such reason will necessarily be a nonscientific evaluative judgment that human beings at early stages of development lack intrinsic value and moral standing. This is the type of judgment that we addressed in chapters four and five, in arguing that all human beings are persons with a right to life. But it is important to acknowledge what kind of argument this is: making a pseudoscientific discrimination between two "kinds" of life, or two "kinds" of human being merely smuggles in moral considerations under the guise of scientific respectability.

So far, then, we have found little convincing evidence for the claim, newly made and defended by supporters of embryo research, that the human embryo is not a human being. The embryo is possessed of a unified life characteristic of very young members of the human species. It is not a part, nor is it in any way analogous to a somatic cell or gametic cell. And it is not, prior to developing the immediately exercisable capacity for sensation or thought, a different kind of entity, a "vegetative" life-form, that only later becomes transformed into a "sentient" or "sapient" life-form. Rather, to this point, we have shown that the evidence clearly supports a quite different, but simple and straightforward claim: human embryos are, from the beginning, human beings.

CHAPTER 7

Further Challenges

. . . . . .

Chapter six began our investigation and refutation of the views of those thinkers who deny that the human embryo is in truth an embryonic human being. It is perhaps worth noting that this challenge is a relatively recent one. Twenty years ago, there were philosophers who tried to establish that human embryos are not persons; but few denied the claim, supported by a solid consensus of human embryological authorities, that the human embryo is a human being. Such denials were more typically made in obviously politicized settings and newspaper editorials, where human embryos and even late-term fetuses were spoken of as "potential human life." It is perhaps somewhat suspicious that this new claim about "potential human life" has more or less coincided with the rise in interest in experimentation on early human embryos.

We showed in chapter six that, contrary to these recent challenges, the human embryo possesses a biologically unified life. We showed further that the possibility of twinning cannot legitimately be taken to mean that the human embryo somehow fails to be a human individual. And we rejected Professor Lee Silver's distinction between the vegetative and sentient "forms of life" that an embryo allegedly moves through, changing its ontological status as it goes. In this chapter, we address two further challenges to the claim that the early human embryo is a complete human being in an early stage of its life.

The first challenge comes from Professor Michael Sandel, of Harvard University, who has denied the humanity of the embryo on the basis of an analogy with acorns and oak trees. The second comes from Dr. Paul McHugh of Johns Hopkins University, who, while accepting that human embryos that are generated from male and female gametes are human beings, denies that "clonotes," that is, embryos that are the result of human cloning, are human beings. Contrary to both Sandel and McHugh, however, we will show that all human embryos, regardless of their age or procreative origin, are human beings.

This will conclude our discussion of the humanity of the early embryo. We will, however, address two further challenges to our view in this chapter before concluding our argument in chapter eight. The authors of these challenges, Professor Ronald Green of Dartmouth College, and Professor Gene Outka of Yale University, have both recently argued that even were one to grant much of what the defender of the human embryo wishes to assert about humanity, personhood, and the ethics of killing, this need not lead to the conclusion that destructive research on human embryos at the beginning of their lives is morally wrong. Green argues that the researchers need not be complicit in the destruction of the embryos; and Outka argues that a principle that he dubs the "nothing is lost" principle can permit research on embryos that would otherwise have been destroyed or discarded. Because these views purport to grant much to the defender of embryonic life, it is worth addressing the challenges they raise here, at the end of our sustained defense of our position.

ACORNS AND EMBRYOS

In an essay in the *New England Journal of Medicine*, Michael Sandel challenged the position that we have here defended, claiming that human embryos are in fact different *in kind* from human beings at later developmental stages.[1] At the core of Sandel's argument is an analogy:

> . . . although every oak tree was once an acorn, it does not follow that acorns are oak trees, or that I should treat the loss of an acorn eaten by a squirrel in my front yard as the same kind of loss as the death of an oak tree felled by a storm. Despite their developmental continuity, acorns and oak trees are different kinds of things.[2]

Sandel maintains that, just as acorns are not oak trees, neither are human embryos human beings; and he concludes that just as we do not value acorns as we value oak trees, neither need we value embryos as we value adult human beings. So Sandel's analogy contains both an ontological and a moral claim. But the analogy, we shall show, is flawed, and thus the argument collapses under scrutiny.

We must first attend to the moral claim by noting a crucial

difference between how we value oak trees and how we value human beings. We will then be in a better position to address the ontological analogy between acorns and embryos. As Sandel concedes, we value human beings precisely because of the *kind* of entities they are. This is a point we have made repeatedly and defended throughout this book. We have argued, indeed, that all human beings are equal in human dignity and human rights, precisely because these are predicated on *what human beings are*, rather than on what they have achieved, or what we have seen fit to bestow upon them.

But this is not an adequate picture of the way we value oak trees. If oak trees were valuable in virtue of the *kind* of entity they are, then it would follow that it is just as unfortunate to lose an acorn as an oak tree (although our emotional reactions to the two different kinds of loss might, for a variety of reasons, nevertheless differ). In fact, we value them because of certain accidental features they have, such as their magnificence—a certain grandeur that has taken perhaps seventy-five or one hundred years to achieve—or their sentimental value, or for the shade they provide in the summer.

Sandel's analogy works, however, only if he disregards the key proposition asserted by opponents of embryo killing, and which we have labored to defend: that all human beings, irrespective of age, size, stage of development, or condition of dependency, possess equal and intrinsic dignity by virtue of what kind of entity they are, and not by virtue of any accidental characteristics, which can come and go, and which are present in human beings in varying degrees. Oak trees are not equally valuable, because the basis for their value is not what they are, but precisely those accidental characteristics by which they differ from acorns: magnificence, or sentimental value, or the shade they provide in the summer.

Professor Sandel's argument begins to go awry with his choice of analogates. The acorn is analogous to the embryo, and the oak tree (he says) to the human being. But in view of the developmental continuity that science fully establishes, and which Sandel concedes, the proper analogate of the oak tree is the mature human being, the adult. Of course, Sandel's analogy has its force because we really do feel a sense of loss when a mature oak is felled. But while it is true that we do not feel the same sense of loss at the destruction of an acorn, it is also true that we do not feel the same sense of loss at the destruction of an oak sapling.

Indeed, our reaction to the destruction of a sapling is much more like our reaction to the destruction of an acorn than to the destruction of a mature oak. But clearly the oak tree does not differ in kind from the oak sapling. And this shows that we value oak trees not because of the kind of entity they are, but rather because of their magnificence, sentimental value, and so on. Acorns and saplings do not have these accidental properties yet, and so we do not experience the same sense of loss when they are destroyed. But if Sandel's analogy were on the mark, the same would be true of our reactions to the death of young children—we would respond to their deaths as we respond to the deaths of saplings, immature members of a species whose accidental properties we happen to value.

As we have stressed, however, this is not the basis at all for our valuing of human beings. We most certainly do not think that especially magnificent human beings, such as Michael Jordan or Albert Einstein, are of greater fundamental and inherent worth and dignity than human beings who are physically frail, or mentally impaired, or even just physically immature. We would not tolerate the killing of a retarded child, or a person suffering from, say, brain cancer, in order to harvest transplantable organs to save Jordan or Einstein.

And we do not tolerate the killing of infants, *which in Sandel's analogy would be analogous to the oak saplings at whose destruction we feel no particular sense of loss*. Managers of oak forests freely kill saplings, just as they might destroy acorns, to ensure the health of the more mature trees. No one regrets this, or gives it a second thought. This is because we simply do not value members of the oak species—as we value human beings—because of the *kind* of entity they are. If we did, then we would likely feel a sense of loss at the destruction of saplings, and it would be reasonable to feel a similar sense of loss at the destruction of acorns. Conversely, if we valued human beings in a way analogous to that in which we value oak trees, then we would have no reason to object to killing human infants or even mature human beings who were severely "defective." Sandel's analogy thus brings into focus—contrary to his intention—the profound difference between the basis on which we value oak trees and the basis on which we ascribe intrinsic value and dignity to human beings.

A second problem with Sandel's argument, which brings us to the metaphysical claims he wishes to defend, is that it relies upon an equivocation on the terms *oak tree* and *human being*. Of course, as Sandel says, acorns are not oak trees—if by *oak tree* one means a *mature member* of the oak species. By the same token, a sapling is also not an "oak tree," if that is what one means by the name. But if by *oak tree* (or *oak*) one means simply any member of the species, then an acorn (or a sapling) is an oak tree (or oak).

They are, after all, identical substances, differing only in maturity or stage of natural development.

Similarly, no one claims that embryos are mature human beings, that is, adults. But they are, as we have shown, human beings, complete though immature members of the human species. So to say, as Sandel does, that embryos and human beings are different kinds of things, or that acorns and oaks are different kinds of things, is true only if one focuses exclusively on accidental characteristics—size, shape, degree of development, and so on. But this is not how biological taxonomy works: we do not identify the species "oak," or "human being," only by reference to mature members of that species, for what we are seeking to identify by the notion of a species is not some set of accidental characteristics, but rather the essential nature shared by some set of beings across various stages of development.

When Sandel claims, therefore, that embryos are not "full human beings," or that they are merely "potential human life," he is trading on an equivocation. For the facts of embryogenesis that we identified in chapter two make clear that human embryos are potential adults, but full—actual—human beings. So in the end, the analogy between oaks and acorns fails: it shows neither that we should not value embryos as we value adult human beings, nor that embryos are not precisely the same kind of beings as the later adult human beings they become.

Perhaps with these facts in mind, Sandel sometimes seems to make one more slide, for he appears at times to concede that human embryos are human beings as a matter of biological fact. Similarly, he says that the oak tree was once an acorn, which would be true only if there were an essential identity shared between the two. But when Sandel speaks in this way, his biological concessions are accompanied by a familiar denial: the denial that human embryos are persons.

In other words, Sandel has recourse to the view that we addressed in chapter five, according to which, although we were once human embryos, we were not "persons" at the time, and were not entitled to the respect and protection against lethal violence due to persons. We became persons, thinks Sandel, only when we became "capable of experience and consciousness," and thus able to "make higher claims" than other human beings who lack these capacities.

To reiterate, briefly, the argument of chapter five, it is clear that personhood is not an accidental characteristic that one may gain and lose at various points in one's life. To be a person is to be an individual who has the basic natural capacity to shape his or her life, by reason and free choice, even though that natural capacity may not be immediately exercisable (as when someone is in a coma), or may take months or years to become immediately exercisable (as with a human infant, fetus, or embryo), or may be blocked by disease or defect (as in severely retarded persons). If not just sentience, but also being "capable of experience and consciousness" were required to be a person, then it would follow that infants and the comatose would not be persons either. Such a claim rightly strikes us as arbitrary and unfair: on what rational grounds could we rule out infants from the domain of moral respect?

Being a person, then, is not a result of acquired accidental attributes, but is a matter of being a certain type of individual, an individual with a rational nature. But human beings are individuals with a rational nature at every moment of their existence. We all come into being as individuals with a rational nature, and we do not cease to be such individuals until we cease to be, by dying. We did not acquire a rational nature by achieving anything—sentience, sapience, or what have you—but by coming into being. If we are persons now, we were persons right from our beginning; we were never human nonpersons.

Professor Sandel has responded to these arguments, which were originally put forth by Robert P. George with Patrick Lee.[3] In his reply, Sandel seems to beg a new question. He claims that this case against his position rests upon the "quaint" metaphysical distinction between essential and accidental attributes of things. Such a charge would, if successful, be crucial in considering the arguments of this book, for we have relied upon the distinction between substance and accident at various points.

Professor Sandel did not, however, offer any ground for dismissing the distinction as "quaint." Nor did he explain why it should be rejected, or how philosophical (including ethical) reflection and discourse can get along without it. This is a critical point, since Sandel himself concedes that the status of a human embryo hinges on the *kind* of entity it is. His case stands or falls on whether he can make good on his promise to show that human embryos and human beings are different in *kind*. Our critique, by contrast, showed that the differences between human embryos, infants, and adults are not, in fact, differences in kind, but merely differences in stages of development and maturity of beings of the same kind. We also showed that the reason for valuing oak trees, unlike the reason for valuing human beings, has to do not with the kind of entity an oak is, but with characteristics such as magnificence, sentimental value, or shade, characteristics that an entity might lack, yet still be a member of the oak species. In other words, we value oak trees on the basis of accidental characteristics.

Now, does Sandel really want to say that it is arbitrary which qualities or attributes make a human being the kind of being it is, and which do not (i.e., which are "accidental")? Does he really wish to deny our claim that being a complete, distinct member of the species Homo sapiens is central to the kind of entity one is, while being male or female, tall or short, young or old, European, Asian, or African, are not? If he honestly thinks that this distinction is merely "quaint," then he owes us an argument for why we should reject a distinction central to American jurisprudence and, indeed, to the main traditions of Western thought about law, ethics, and their relationship.

As we argued in chapter three, the nature of a being or entity—the kind of thing it is—is established by its characteristic actions and reactions and regular properties. Its other characteristics, such as weight, height, sex, age, race, ethnicity, stage of development, state of mental or physical health, and so on, do not establish its nature, and are in that sense accidental. Does Sandel—or anyone else, for that matter—seriously doubt that he would have remained himself had he entered room A rather than room B? And does this not prove that the place an entity is in is an accidental attribute?

Moreover, has not Professor Sandel, like the authors and readers of this book, endured through time, proving that age also is an accidental attribute? The distinction between what Professor Sandel is, essentially—a human being—and what he is accidentally—so-and-so many years old, or a resident of such-and-such a location—is far from being "quaint."

Similarly, the magnificence of an oak tree, an attribute it has only, if all goes well, with maturation, cannot reasonably be considered to establish the *kind* of thing the oak tree is. An oak sapling, on any reasonable account, is the same kind of entity, differing from the mature tree only in respect of its stage of development. The entity that began as an acorn, became a sapling, and eventually developed to full maturity is a unitary and determinate entity that endured over time. It persisted through the different stages of its development—from acorn, to sapling, to full maturity. If the analogy of acorn to embryo shows anything, at a biological or metaphysical level, it shows that the human being, like the oak tree, started out small; but that differences of size, like myriad other differences, are irrelevant to what that early human embryo was.

CLONOTES?

Unlike Sandel, Dr. Paul McHugh acknowledges that early human embryos that are the result of sexual reproduction or in vitro fertilization are human beings. But McHugh accompanies this acknowledgment with what seems to us a very peculiar denial. For McHugh believes that those embryos (which he calls "clonotes") that come into being as the result of Somatic Cell Nuclear Transfer—cloning—are different *in kind* from those embryos that come into being as a result of the union of male and female gametes. In other words, McHugh denies that clonotes are human beings.

Here is McHugh's argument in his own words:

> Thus, I argue that in vitro fertilization entails the begetting of a new human being right from its start as a zygote and that we should use it to produce babies rather than cells or tissues to be harvested for purposes dictated by other human beings. In contrast SCNT is a biological manufacturing process that we may use to produce cells but should not use to produce babies.[4]

The conditions of origin thus make, for McHugh, an ontological difference, rendering "clonotes" different in kind from early human embryos.

The trouble with this argument is that the "clonote" and the "embryo," despite the different processes by which they come into being, are indistinguishable biologically. What McHugh rightly says about the in vitro fertilization process, namely, that it "creates a new human being right from its start as a zygote," is also true of the entity produced by Somatic Cell Nuclear Transfer (SCNT). All the characteristics of the embryo are to be found in the "clonote." Indeed, there is no point in inventing a new word. As the vast majority of people on both sides of the debate over embryo ethics understand perfectly well, what Somatic Cell Nuclear Transfer produces is a cloned embryo.

McHugh says that his "distinction rests on the origin of the cells in SCNT, not on the process's vaunted potential for producing a living replica (clone) of the donor, as with Dolly the sheep."

But, of course, Dolly the sheep began her life as an embryonic sheep. She did not skip the embryonic stage. In this respect, she was indistinguishable from other sheep. Similarly, a human adult brought into existence by Somatic Cell Nuclear Transfer would have begun his life as a human embryo. The potential he fulfilled—namely, the potential to develop from the embryonic into and through the fetal, infant, child, and adolescent stages, and into adulthood—would be the potential he possessed from the embryonic stage forward.

Similarly, it is inaccurate to say that the embryonic Dolly had the "potential" to be a living replica of the sheep from which she was cloned. From the embryonic stage forward, she *was* a living replica of the sheep from which she was cloned. There was no separate entity, the sheep "clonote," that had the potential to become a sheep. There was only a very immature sheep whose origin was, at the time, rather unusual.

Just as the life of a new human being conceived by sexual union develops by a gradual and gapless process during which the developing human being never changes from one kind of entity into another, so too the life of a human being produced by Somatic Cell Nuclear Transfer would unfold without what philosophers call substantial change—a change from being one kind of entity to being another kind. In the life of such a being, there would be no point from the embryonic stage forward at which one could say that the developing being changed from a nonhuman entity into a human being. From the point at which SCNT succeeded in producing a distinct, self-integrating organism, a new human being existed.

McHugh attempts to support his position with an argument in the form of a reductio ad absurdum:

> . . . if one used the notion of "potential" to protect cells
> developed through SCNT because with further manipula-
> tion they might become a living clone, then every somatic
> cell would deserve some protection because it has the po-
> tential to follow the same path.[5]

But this argument, as we have already shown, fails. Somatic cells that may be used in cloning are not analogous to embryos, but to gametes. Functionally, they are parts of other human beings. They are not distinct, complete, self-integrating organisms. They are not members of the species Homo sapiens. But human embryos, by whatever method they are generated, are.

In fact, it is McHugh's argument that is most vulnerable to a reductio ad absurdum. If a "clonote" is not an embryonic member of the species of the animal from which it is cloned, then even in the adult stage, the cloned entity cannot be a member of that species. So Dolly was in fact not a sheep, and the child, and later adult, who had begun life as a "clonote" would not be a human being. This conclusion is absurd. But it follows from McHugh's claim about the nature of the "clonote," in conjunction with basic biological facts about the development of that "clonote." For the adult clone was once, those biological facts show, that cloned embryo.

McHugh has one more argument. Relying on testimony given by Rudolph Jaenisch at the July 24, 2003, meeting of the President's Council on Bioethics, McHugh asserts that "SCNT performed with primate cells produces embryos with such severe epigenetic problems that they cannot survive to birth."[6] The first thing to notice about this assertion is that it concedes that the entities produced by SCNT are, in fact, embryos, albeit severely disabled ones. More important, Jaenisch's testimony does nothing to prove that disabled or "defective" embryos lack moral worth. As we mentioned in chapter six, in some cases reproduction fails because fertilization is incomplete, and in such a case, there is a growth (for example, a complete hydatidiform mole), but there is no human embryo. But if SCNT is successful, then it generates a distinct organism with the full genetic program and active disposition to develop itself in accord with that program, even if it has some defect that will cause its early death.

Similarly, there are newborn infants who, as a result of genetic diseases, are destined to die in a matter of days or even hours. This fact does not alter their status as human beings. It would be scandalous to suppose that it authorizes us to treat such afflicted children as impersonal collections of organs available for transplantation and research.

Human beings may be severely afflicted at any developmental stage, from the embryonic to the adult. All of us will eventually die, and many of us will die as a result of factors characterizing our genetic makeup from the point at which we came into being. From the moral point of view, the certainty of death—whether in ninety years or nine minutes—does not alter our inherent dignity or relieve others of obligations to respect our lives. That someone will soon die, no matter what we do, is never a license for killing him. That the human being whose death is imminent happens to be at an earlier or later stage of development is morally irrelevant. And that he or she came into existence this way rather than that way is scarcely any more relevant.

All these points tell against McHugh's claims. But they serve as well as a transition to the final arguments of this book, with which we will close this chapter. For while McHugh argued—unsuccessfully, as we have shown—that the inevitable early death of the cloned human embryo rendered it other than a human being, others have argued that the inevitable early death of the many human embryos currently cryopreserved, and destined to be discarded or killed, provides justification for using those embryos for research, including destructive research. These arguments pose the final challenge to the view we have defended in this book, and to these arguments we now turn.

"NOTHING IS LOST" AND "NO COOPERATION WITH EVIL"

Suppose that one granted much that we have said about the ontological status of human embryos. In particular, suppose one granted that human embryos are human beings, and that the readers and authors of this book, and all others essentially like them, are human beings. Suppose further that one granted at least much of the moral picture we have presented, and refused, at any rate, to accept some form of consequentialism. Suppose one even accepted that early human beings possessed intrinsic worth or personal dignity. Could one accept all this, or much of it, and still hold it morally permissible to engage in destructive research on early human embryos?

We have argued that one could not reasonably hold this view. For all human beings are human persons and are to be respected as such by promoting and preserving in them those human goods constitutive of their well-being, including the good of human life. We argued that because there exists a moral norm prohibiting the intentional taking of the life of an innocent human being, there was also a correlative rights claim, a claim to a right not to be intentionally killed. All human beings, we argued, were subjects of precisely this sort of right.

Nevertheless, there are circumstances in which proponents of the sort of ethics that we have defended have, almost unanimously, held that it is morally permissible to use lethal force. For example, it is almost universally accepted that it is permissible to use force to repel a violent attack in order to preserve one's own life or the lives of others. So one might think that the moral prohibition on killing can be overridden in some circumstances.

However, two features stand out in cases such as those just presented. The first is that the person against whom lethal force may be used is one who is an aggressor posing a threat; they are attacking someone, and must be stopped. This is far, then, from the sort of permission given by utilitarians and other consequentialists for killing for the sake of some good to be obtained.

The second feature of justifications for the use of lethal force against attackers, traditional among proponents of the sort of ethics we have defended, is that the lethal effect of the use of force in defense must itself not be intended by the person defending him- or herself. That is to say, the defender has an end that she pursues: to preserve her life. And she has a means she has chosen: to ward off the attacker with Mace, or with a knife, or with a gun. But she does not, precisely, choose to kill in order to preserve her life. Rather, she chooses to ward off, aware that a consequence of using a gun to do this might, as it probably would not using Mace, be the death of her attacker.

This line of thought has been extended by many thinkers, however, to other contexts of killing in ways that make the death of those who are not attacking one permissible. So, in war, the military might bomb a strategic arms depot, knowing that some innocent—i.e., nonattacking—civilians who live nearby might unavoidably be killed. But because their deaths are held to be a side effect, and not intended by the military, they are accepted as "collateral damage," and not viewed as exceptions to the prohibition against killing the innocent. Importantly, these sorts of justification are not consequentialist, nor do they require a denial that those killed are persons with a right to life. Rather, they maintain a strict prohibition against intentional killing of those who pose no threat.

Still, it remains the case that even an ethic with a strict prohibition on intentional killing of the innocent permits some lethal use of force under some circumstances, as in, again, the case of those who are attacking, and those killed collaterally. Can such, or similar, extensions be applied in the case of embryonic research to permit human embryo killing within an ethic that accepts that they are persons with a right to life? Recently, some philosophers and theologians have tried to do just this, arguing from within a putatively traditional moral framework to the conclusion that at least some embryos may permissibly be subjects of lethal experimentation. Let us examine the arguments of two prominent ethicists.

The first argument is that of Gene Outka, a professor of philosophy and Christian ethics at Yale University. Professor Outka has proposed that a maxim that he calls the "nothing-is-lost" principle can be extended from certain kinds of conflict cases to cover the case of embryos who are slated to be destroyed or abandoned so as to allow for their being used in medical research.

The nothing-is-lost principle, as understood by Outka, is intended to permit the use of lethal force in cases of conflict. In Outka's formulation, "One may directly kill when two conditions obtain: (a) the innocent will die in any case; and (b) other innocent life will be saved."[7] In the case of embryos, Outka wishes to extend the principle in the following way: One may directly kill if "(a) nothing more is lost, and (b) less is lost, or at least someone is saved."[8]

Thus, in the case of embryos left over from IVF, research upon which might be useful to saving lives, Outka writes, "They will die, unimplanted, in any case. (Nothing more will be lost by their becoming subjects of research.)"[9] Thus Outka's conclusion, that, since some lives might be saved, and nothing will be lost, it is permissible to experiment on embryos already alive, but without any hope of being brought to maturation. But, by the same token, it is impermissible to create embryos for the sake of such experimentation. For in this case, bringing them into being in order to perform destructive research upon them is not a case of nothing being lost; we would be creating precisely in order to destroy.

Now, we should note two aspects of Outka's defense of destructive embryo research. The first is that Outka frames his nothing-is-lost principle as justifying intentional killing (which he calls "direct" killing). This makes his defense slightly different from the defense of lethal force against an attacker that we described above. The second is that Outka claims to "take conception and all that it alone makes possible as *the* point at which one should ascribe a judgment of irreducible value. Once conceived, each entity is a form of primordial human life, a being in its own right, that should exert a claim upon others to be regarded as an end rather than a mere means *only*."[10] This sounds on the surface of it rather similar to the view that we have defended. But, as we shall show, nothing like Outka's nothing-is-lost principle could apply were this the case; and, in fact, on scrutiny, his view of early human embryos turns out to be rather different from ours.

Consider one of the few examples that Outka gives of a case of the nothing-is-lost principle in action. In a lifeboat with too many occupants, "we can choose whom we may save, but we cannot save both, or we cannot save all."[11] Or consider a similar case in which there is not enough medicine to cure all suffering from a lethal disease. In such cases of conflict it is true that a choice may be made; we must save some, for it would be foolish and immoral simply to let everyone perish. But these are certainly not cases of directly killing. Rather, in saving one, an agent foresees that others will die; but few would ever say that the agent thereby *kills* those he does not—and is not able to—save.

But now consider a case of direct killing of one slated to die: we might harvest the organs of a terminally ill patient, or a comatose person, or a criminal on death row. These are certainly cases of direct or intentional killing, and it would seem that nothing is lost, and indeed, something is gained: we might save many lives with the organs of those whose deaths will come soon anyway. But in these cases, Outka resists application of the nothing-is-lost principle, citing the "specter of Nazi doctors." But what grounds can there be for resisting, if one sees the principle as licensing direct killing under the conditions described by Outka?

The answer is, as it happens, not difficult to find. For despite the rhetoric of "irreducible value" that Outka applies to early embryos, it is clear that he does not, in the end, think of them as human persons ontologically and morally on par with the readers and authors of this book. Rather,

> [b]efore individualization and implantation, the entity does not yet have the full-fledged moral standing of a fetus. Yet, for its part, a fetus's value is not equally protectable with the pregnant woman's, for she too is an end in herself and has developed beyond the potentiality that still charac-terizes the fetus. Equal protectability holds after the fetus becomes capable of independent existence outside the womb.[12]

This denial of equal protectability is in turn buttressed by a claim Outka makes about the metaphysical status of excess embryos. Such embryos, he says, are doomed to a "perpetual po-tentiality," which "leads us intelligibly to find more affinities than differences between fetal cadavers and the embryos in ques-tion."[13] Here, at any rate, we are on familiar ground. For the per-petual potentiality that an early embryo who is unfortunate enough to have been cryopreserved possesses is the potentiality for maturation, for childhood, for adulthood, and so on. But this perpetual potentiality is certainly not such as to render the early embryo more like than unlike a cadaver (or a dog or a cat). This perpetual potentiality does not eliminate what will be a perpet-ual actuality, at least as long as the embryo continues to live, namely, the actuality of being a living individual of the human species.

In the end, then, Outka's argument depends upon the

same errors regarding potentiality that we have seen before. And it is clear that if he did not make these errors, he would be disinclined to frame his nothing-is-lost principle in terms of direct killing. For when it comes to cases in which he is convinced of the full humanity of the being who is doomed to die, as in the case of the comatose, the terminally ill, or the convicted criminal, he does not endorse the principle, although, as he expresses it, it is manifestly applicable. And in this, Outka shows his good sense, for it is repugnant to morality to think that those whose deaths are impending may therefore be directly killed if some benefit can thereby be achieved. Only consequentialists would be willing to make such a claim about the lives of human persons.

This suggests that the only available line of retreat is to endorse the claim that the destruction of embryos in scientific research need *not* be a case of intentional killing. And this is, indeed, the approach suggested by Ronald Green, in an attempt to find a compromise between supporters and opponents of destructive embryo research.

We should note, first, that Green's expressed opinion is not, as is Outka's, that early human embryos have irreducible value, nor does he think that they are human persons. Indeed, as we saw in an earlier chapter, Green does not think that early human embryos are human beings at all. Rather, as we saw, he holds that both biological and moral judgments are matters of decision. There are no bright lines in either area of inquiry.

Moreover, Green thinks that the stakes are sufficiently high that our judgment regarding the humanity of the embryo, and the morality of killing it, should be quite permissive. Green supports, as Outka does not, the creation of embryos for research purposes, in addition to experimentation on so-called "spare" embryos. Nevertheless, in an article in the journal *Bioethics*, Green suggested an argument that he believed might persuade those who were convinced of the humanity and personhood of the early embryo that destructive research might be permissible.

Green's argument is framed in terms of a Catholic family's need for stem cell therapy for an ailing child, and their desire neither to involve themselves in the murder of embryos, nor wrongly to benefit from immoral research. As such, it might seem to have application only to those worried after the fact of embryonic destruction about their complicity. In fact, however, the argument seems intended to generate a stronger conclusion: that even those scientists who engage in the research itself need not understand themselves as impermissibly engaged in the killing.

Much of Green's argument attempts to set out the conditions under which it would be permissible to benefit from impermissible research. Green identifies three circumstances that would make it wrong. The first is if the benefiting involves directly encouraging the wrongful research "through agency." In such a case, the one who wants the benefit asks someone else to, as it were, do the dirty work himself. A second case of wrongly benefiting occurs when accepting the benefits directly encourages those doing the research to continue. And a third involves indirect encouragement of the practice; in this case, the original immoral researchers might no longer be alive to be encouraged, but benefiting from their results encourages that sort of research by others, even if it does not encourage those original researchers.

Green then contrasts an obvious case of legitimate benefiting from wrongdoing with the stem cell case. Could the Catholic family accept organs donated by the family of a boy shot in a gang-related killing? Yes, Green plausibly suggests, because "None of our three forms of encouragement are present in this case."[14] Nothing that is done will have any impact one way or another on the problem of gang-related shootings, so it is permissible to accept the organs.

The embryonic research case would seem to be considerably different, though, for it "appears to violate two, and in some cases, all three of these encouragement considerations."[15] But this, Green argues, is a mistake:

> The key insight here is that . . . embryo destruction is entirely independent of hESC [human embryonic stem cell] research and therapy. Surplus embryos are routinely created in the practice of infertility medicine. . . . This will not change until the distant future. . . . Until then, thousands of embryos will be produced each year in hundreds of infertility clinics around the world, and, eventually, many of these embryos will be destroyed when couples are no longer willing—or available—to pay for the embryos' continued cryopreservation.[16]

Thus, Green asks, and answers:

> Do those who use hESC lines employ as agents those who destroy the embryos needed to create them? Not unless they expressly authorize the creation of an embryo for this purpose. Does using an hESC line indirectly encourage progenitors (or researchers working with them) to authorize the destruction of an embryo? No, because this destruction is undertaken for separate and independent reasons and will likely continue to be so. Does use of hESC

lines indirectly encourage such destruction by creating a practice that legitimizes the destruction of human embryos in the future? . . . [No, for] whatever some people choose to do, the massive creation and destruction of embryos will continue.[17]

Now again, we might think that this conclusion concerns only the ultimate beneficiaries of embryonic research. But in fact, Green does not think that the researchers on embryonic stem cells participate in the destruction of those embryos either, even when they directly "dissolve the trophoblast and expose the inner cell mass."[18] For "hESC research using any of the thousands of embryos slated for destruction does not *cause* the death of those embryos; the decision to discard them does that. Research causes only the *manner* of their destruction; however, we can see that this is morally unimportant."[19]

Green, like Outka, holds that these conclusions follow only in the case of "spare" embryos, and do not carry over to the case of embryo creation for destructive research. But it is clear that even researchers morally opposed to embryo killing could participate in destructive research, since they would not be responsible for the embryos' deaths; presumably only the parents of the embryos would be so responsible.

This is a very striking claim. But it is, on the surface, rather implausible. Consider the German physician in the Nazi period who is ordered to euthanize a handicapped child under the eugenics program. Is it true of him that he does not cause the child's death, that only those who made the decision are genuinely responsible? Moreover, suppose that there was some scientific purpose that could be achieved only by filling the child's lungs with fluid. Was the scientist who requested that the victim be killed in that way, rather than, say, by lethal injection, only making a request about the manner of death, and therefore not responsible for the death itself? Such conclusions are repugnant. Indeed, we would think that physicians and scientists had a grave moral responsibility to refuse to participate at all.

What, then, could make such an argument seem attractive and plausible? Only, we believe, a previously drawn conclusion to the effect that early human embryos are not, after all, human beings and persons, subjects of fundamental human rights. It is only if we bracket this key claim that we can observe with Green's detachment the "difference" between causing the death of the embryos and causing the manner of the embryos' deaths. In any parallel case involving recognized persons, this would seem the classic case of a distinction without a difference.

Of course, Green's points about the wider context within which embryonic research is proposed are important. It certainly should be a matter of considerable moral concern that a widespread and largely unregulated industry exists, one function of which is to create "spare" human beings, who will be either perpetually cryopreserved, or abandoned and destroyed. We shall address this issue briefly in chapter eight. But the response to widespread moral wrongdoing and gross injustice should never be acquiescence or accommodation; where innocent human lives are at stake, such moral passivity is unacceptable.

We do not think, then, that if one attends squarely to the claim that early human embryos are human beings with full human rights, one could endorse either Outka's or Green's proposals for legitimizing destructive research on human embryos. Let us offer one further reconstruction of an argument, using the distinctions drawn earlier in the discussion concerning indirect killing. Could one argue that the production of stem cells by means involving embryo destruction is itself not a case of direct killing at all, but only the removal of cells for research, with the foreseen side effect that the embryos would die?

Here is Green's description of the process:

> Normally, embryos are disposed of by being exposed to alcohol or a similar agent and then incinerated. But when a blastocyst is to be used as a source of hESCs, it is kept alive until immunosurgery procedures are applied to it in order to dissolve the trophoblast and expose the inner cell mass.[20]

Certainly Green's description of the ordinary procedure of "disposal" makes it clear that the intention is precisely to eliminate the embryo, i.e., to kill it. But perhaps one could make the case that the surgical procedure he describes really does have as its end scientific progress, and as its means, the removal of certain cells, without the researcher intending the death of the embryo as such.

Nonetheless, it is important to realize that even when a negative effect is "outside" the scope of an agent's intention, or is merely collateral to some otherwise noble end, other considerations retain their moral weight. In particular, it is typically not right—because not fair—to ask some to share the burdensome effects of an act that will exclusively benefit others. So even if the removal of vital organs from a homeless vagabond, for the sake of saving many, was not an instance of direct killing of the vagabond, still, it is manifestly unfair to demand of him the sacrifice of his organs, or his life, for people to whom he has no obligations, and from whom he will receive no benefits.

Similarly, it seems manifestly unfair to take from humans in the embryonic stage, who are innocent if anyone is, what is necessary for their sustained life, in order to benefit anonymous others, to whom the embryo has no connection, and from whom they will receive no benefit. And even if those to be benefited are the embryo's parents, the situation still strikes us as asymmetrical and unfair: parents, after all, undertake responsibilities to their children by bringing them into existence, not the other way around. For parents to make use of their children, even in their embryonic stages, seems, again, grossly unfair to these most vulnerable of members of the human family.

In consequences, even if some instance of embryonic research that had the death of an embryo as its consequence was not a case of intentional killing of the embryo, it would still be wrongful because it is an unfair imposition of burden on an innocent human being. We conclude then that destructive research on human embryos cannot be morally justified. Human beings have a moral right not to be intentionally killed to benefit others. This right obtains for human beings by virtue of what they are, namely, creatures with a rational nature. It is not possessed by some human beings but not by others. It is possessed by all human beings and is possessed by them from the time they come into being. It is a *human* right.

CHAPTER 8

Conclusion

. . . . . .

We have defended, in the course of this book, three important claims, all central to a correct understanding of the ethics of embryonic research. First, human embryos are human beings, and every product of successful fertilization is a human being. Second, we, the readers and authors of this book, and all other beings that are essentially like us, are human beings; we are not disembodied souls, and while we are, indeed, persons, this should not be interpreted as meaning that we are something other than human beings. Rather, all human beings are persons, from the beginning of their existence, because human beings lead personal lives. Third, because all human beings are persons, all human beings are subjects of absolute human rights, including the right not to be intentionally killed.

It follows from these claims that any scientific research conducted on embryonic humans, and destructive of their life or health, is wrong, immoral, unjust. No scientist, or any other agent, should ever willingly engage in activities that would deliberately threaten the life or health of human beings at any stage of development or in any condition.

This conclusion, however, raises many important questions, three of which we shall characterize as the Political Question, the Technological Question, and the Cultural Question. The questions are complex, and intertwined with one another, and we cannot hope adequately to address them here, in our concluding chapter. But we wish to indicate the directions that we believe adequate answers to these questions would go in. In what follows, we discuss these questions, and put forth in response several proposals that we believe will take our country farther down the road to justice for early human life.

THE POLITICAL QUESTION

The critical political question that emerges from our argument is this: given that destructive research on early human life is a form of wrongful killing, what should be the appropriate response on the part of the state? This question is made difficult by the popularity of political theories according to which it would be wrong for the state to prohibit embryo-destructive research, even if the judgment that such research is morally wrong is correct. According to such theories, species of what is termed by its advocates "political liberalism," it is wrong for the state to prohibit an activity over which there is significant or "reasonable" moral disagreement, or in which individuals had a significant interest in determining their own personal meanings and values. Leading political liberals argue that it is wrong to restrict basic liberties on the basis of judgments drawn from "comprehensive" religious or philosophical doctrines, even if the judgments are true.[1]

Let us first dispense with one instance of this view that we believe is hardly worth comment. We have already seen, in chapter one, the claim of Professor Lee Silver that views and arguments such as ours are inherently religious. Similarly, Ronald Green claims, in his book *The Human Embryo Research Debates*, that the "prolife" view has its essential roots in religion. Accordingly, both authors believe, it follows that no pro-embryo view can serve as a valid basis for legislation, for this would be to violate the separation of church and state.

Yet what could be a more obvious mischaracterization of the claims of this book? We have relied upon science, and upon moral philosophy, true. But at no point have we relied upon revealed religious doctrine, or ecclesiastical authority of any type. If there is religious prejudice, it is not to be found in this book, but in the arguments of those whose hostility to religion causes them to see its influence in virtually any judgment that does not line up with their own convictions or preferences. To claim that arguments like those we advance deserve no place in public discussion about embryo policy on the grounds of church-state separation is silly.

Similarly misguided would be a claim that injustice to human embryos is a "private" matter, not appropriate for public policy. Similar claims have been made, of course, about abortion. In reply, two points should be made. First, and this is true of abortion as well, it is difficult to see how any form of killing of human beings could properly be considered a "private" matter. By the nature of the case, two individuals are involved; moreover, in this particular type of case, one of the individuals does not consent. Most important, killing is essentially a violation of the most basic form of community available to human beings, a community that is prepolitical, but inescapably "public."

Second, embryo killing for research is public in more visible ways as well, and in this it is rather unlike abortion. It is proposed that human embryo-destructive research be done with public money, in public facilities, by members of the deeply public profession of science. It is not a matter of personal choice, but of public policy. To claim that it is part of a protected sphere of privacy is absurd.

According to another, and more sophisticated, variation of these views, one with roots in the work of the late John Rawls, it is not necessary that a view be rooted in religion, or private, in order for it rightly to be excluded from the public sphere and political debate. But neither is it sufficient that the truth of the view be available to natural reason for the view to be an acceptable ground of public policy. According to defenders of this view, it is not germane that the conclusion for which we have argued in this book is true, or the most reasonable, or the best argued. Rather, as Judith Jarvis Thomson has argued in defending the right to abortion, what matters is that defenders of that right are "not unreasonable" in disagreeing with the claims of those who defend the rights of the unborn.[2]

In consequence of this, it is concluded, views such as ours are incapable of being defended with "public reason." Defenders of such views are therefore themselves unreasonable in attempting to make them the bases for public policy.

We agree that public reason is an important value in public deliberation. Policy decisions should not be made on the basis of secrets known only by the elect, nor should they promote private or exclusively sectarian causes. But we have not relied on or advanced reasons of this sort. On any plausible interpretation of public reason, our argument in this book should pass muster. So what can be meant by saying that the fact of "reasonable disagreement" shows that our arguments are not within the bounds of public reason?

One interpretation of "reasonable disagreement" clearly will not do. One might hold that every significant moral or political disagreement is reasonable simply because there is no true position, or sound argument to make. Such a view would be a straightforward case of relativism. But relativism is hardly a secure basis on which to build a just polity: if every position is as good as another, and every truth claim equally true, then there would seem to be nothing but raw power that could serve as a basis for political agreement and decision. But this is quite contrary to the stated intentions of the defenders of political liberalism, who wish precisely to secure a foundation in justice for political debate and decision.

A second interpretation of the fact of reasonable disagreement might go as follows. Even reasonable people sometimes make mistakes, and they are not always in moral error in doing so. Some matters are difficult to appraise judiciously. Moreover, even generally reasonable people can sometimes be affected by bias and prior interest in a matter, without this significantly compromising their moral uprightness. To say this hardly means that those with whom one disagrees are bad people; nor is it to fail to respect them as rational beings. People of goodwill—reasonable people—make mistakes, both moral and nonmoral.

We agree wholeheartedly that reasonable people can disagree, often without moral fault. And we agree that even when disagreement is the result of bias or interest, this need not impugn the entirety of a person's character. But it is precisely because we acknowledge the fact of reasonable disagreement in this sense that we have written this book. It is an attempt to argue with those persons of goodwill—our colleagues, fellow citizens, and friends—who do not agree with our views, but whom we think are open to reasoned argument. Likewise, we hope ourselves to be open to such argument; we will listen and respond to objections to our views, and recognize the possibility that we have gone wrong somewhere in the course of our defense of embryonic human life.

What, however, are the political implications of acknowledging this? As far as we can tell, the only implication is that citizens generally, ourselves and our interlocutors included, should maintain civility and respect in the course of defending their positions, and arguing for the most just possible solutions to political problems. There is no implication that our view, or any like it, should be ruled out of court without being considered on its merits.

This conclusion is unacceptable to the defender of political liberalism, however. For the political liberal, the defender of Rawlsian public reason, wishes to use that concept, and the fact of reasonable disagreement, as a defeater for certain views and arguments without the necessity of considering them on their merits. This, we claim, is a deeply unreasonable position. What could justify the exclusion of a view from public deliberation without argument, without any claim that it was deficient, whether by failing to reach the truth, or by proceeding on the basis of faulty argument?

The political liberal is therefore in a dilemma: either refuse, without argument, to address the merits of the arguments we have put forth; or come to grips directly with those arguments, assessing them for validity and soundness.

Only the latter approach is, we believe, reasonable. Yet suppose that approach were followed. Our interlocutor would, we believe, be forced to concede that embryo-destructive research is the unjust killing of an innocent human being, a violation of a fundamental human right. He would further need to concede that this conclusion was supported by a sound argument, available to natural reason, and not rooted in revelation or esoteric doctrine. But if all this is the case, what could possibly justify a refusal to use the powers of the state to protect embryonic human life by legislation prohibiting embryo killing in scientific research?

Here we move away from abstract questions of "public reason" and "reasonable disagreement" to foundational but very practical questions concerning the political state: What are the purposes of the state, and what may it do to secure those purposes?

Questions about the nature and purpose of the state are, like all the questions in this book, themselves subject to considerable disagreement. Yet we believe the following three claims about the state articulate important truths, and can command widespread assent. First, the state exists to protect all those within its borders from various dangers, both internal and external, and in particular from the aggression of other persons. For defense of the former sort, the state has a police force; for defense of the latter, it has a military force.

Second, the state exists not just to defend, but to promote the well-being of its citizens. This it does not, typically, do directly, but rather by establishing the conditions under which individuals, families, and groups can act together to pursue their well-being. States make these conditions possible in a wide variety of ways: building roads, establishing schools, assisting in the provision of health care, and so on.

Third, a primary instrumentality of the state, and uniquely appropriate to it, in protecting persons and promoting their well-being is the law. In large part this is because the law, by its impersonality and publicity, makes possible the two tasks of the state in a fairer way than could typically be accomplished by merely personal authority. For the rule of law, and not men, makes more difficult the arbitrary assertion of power of one over another, the biased defense of some lives at the expense of others, or a self-interested distribution of benefits that makes possible the pursuit of well-being for some, but not all. Moreover, a public and widely promulgated law gives assurances to all that they will be treated equally, and lets them know of what such equal treatment will consist.

Return, then, to the hypothetical reader of this text who engages with the arguments and becomes convinced of their soundness. If that reader likewise agrees with these three foundational claims about the state, what conclusion can reasonably be drawn? Only that a state that promotes or even allows the destruction of human embryos for the sake of benefits to other citizens fails to live up to its responsibilities precisely as a state: it fails to protect its most defenseless citizens, and it does so in the course of unfairly providing benefits to some persons at the expense of others. In light of these considerations, we therefore submit the following proposal to our readers for their consideration:

The Political Proposal: The United States should acknowledge, in law, the obligation to protect embryonic human life by prohibiting all embryo-destructive research. As a necessary means to this, the United States must maintain its current prohibition on federal funding for such research, and states should adopt similar measures prohibiting taxpayer-funded embryo-destructive research.

THE TECHNOLOGICAL QUESTION

Having addressed the political question and concluded that the state should protect embryonic human beings, just as it protects humans at later developmental stages, we must give some attention to the claims of science, and in particular biomedical research. Stem cell research represents to many scientists a kind of holy grail, an opportunity to expand radically the boundaries of knowledge, and the limits of medical therapy. Scientists and medical researchers are unlikely to be pleased with the limits we have defended.

What, then, can we suggest as alternatives to embryo-destructive research? It is important to note that it is not, strictly speaking, necessary for us to hold out hope of some research program capable of satisfying all the needs that scientists promise embryonic research will satisfy. For there can be little doubt that an ethical engagement in science and medical research sometimes does require sacrifice. Perhaps great strides in curing cancer could be made were we to do lethal experiments on terminally ill cancer patients. Perhaps, overall, more lives could be saved than lost. But such calculations are irrelevant; the moral demand to respect human persons defeats such hopes of the "greater good."

Nevertheless, it is worth pointing to a number of options that remain less than fully explored by scientists, as avenues by which ethically sound and relatively uncontroversial research can be pursued. It is not certain whether any of the options we suggest will, in the end, bear fruit. (It is not certain either, however, whether embryonic stem cell research would bear fruit.) But plainly it would be unreasonable to ignore these possibilities in favor of a dogmatic insistence that only embryonic stem cell research can possibly result in significant benefits.

In chapter one, we pointed to the possibility of adult stem cell therapies as one such avenue. We believe that research of this sort is highly promising. Indeed, many people are already benefiting from it. It also appears to involve no ethical hazards, and this should make it a top priority for those who wish to advance scientific research in a responsible manner. Similarly, recent studies have suggested that stem cells extracted from placental tissue might offer many of the same advantages scientists hope to obtain from embryonic stem cells. But like adult stem cells, they are ethically unproblematic.

We also find encouraging a proposal of some scientists to dedifferentiate adult somatic cells back to a stage of pluripotency, such as that possessed by embryonic stem cells. Recall that as the embryo develops, its cells become specialized by "turning off" various genes. Dedifferentiation would "turn back the clock" on such cells. These pluripotent cells could then be reoriented toward one or another type of differentiated tissue, just as if they were embryonic stem cells. Because this proposal does not involve any making or killing of human embryos, it does not seem to us any more morally problematic than continued research into adult stem cells.

Two other proposals also seem potentially promising, though they engender moral controversy. (We refer readers to the White Paper of the President's Council on Bioethics, "Alternative Sources of Human Pluripotent Stem Cells" for further discussion of the ethical, scientific, and practical implications of these proposals.)[3] One is to extract cells from dead embryos, which have perished subsequent to IVF, in hopes that they would still maintain their pluripotentiality. Although this possibility does not involve killing embryos, it would require a much clearer way than we now possess to determine whether a cryopreserved embryo had indeed died.

A second proposal has been advanced by Dr. William Hurlbut, a member of the President's Council on Bioethics.[4] Dr. Hurlbut believes that with knowledge gained from animal experiments it will soon be possible to manufacture a "biological artifact," ontologically different from an early human being, from which stem cells could be extracted. Hurlbut's proposed procedure is called "altered nuclear transfer (ANT)," and is similar in some ways to somatic cell nuclear transfer, or cloning. In ANT, however, the somatic cell nucleus would be altered before transfer to the enucleated oocyte so as to ensure that the resulting entity "would lack the essential attributes and capacities of a human being."[5] This resulting growth is described, variously, as like a tissue culture, a teratoma, or a hydatidiform mole.

It is essential, if this procedure is to provide a genuine and morally upright alternative to embryo-destructive research, that scientists know for sure that the resulting entity is not an embryo. Some fear that rather than creating a nonembryonic entity, scientists would succeed only in creating a defective or radically damaged human embryo.[6] Moreover, it would be important to determine whether ova could be supplied for the ANT procedure without subjecting women to the painful and possibly dangerous process of hormonal stimulation known as superovulation. But, subject to these qualifications, Dr. Hurlbut's proposal seems potentially meritorious, and could initially be pursued using animal cells and ova without ethical qualms.

The President's Council White Paper discusses a further proposal that we believe is more problematic: the extraction by biopsy of pluripotent stem cells from living embryos. Such biopsies are currently performed on some IVF embryos to determine whether the embryo will suffer from any genetic defects if implanted and permitted to grow and develop. But it is not yet clear whether enough pluripotent cells can be detached from an embryo to be useful without harming the embryo or even causing its death.

More important, however, from an ethical standpoint, is the following consideration. By all recognized norms of research ethics, it is clearly wrong to perform invasive experimental research on an individual, to the degree even of removing a body part, for no therapeutic purpose for that individual, and without informed consent by that individual. The fact that embryos are in no position to provide that informed consent is not the point; we do not believe that the organs of comatose persons can be taken from them, even if in doing so we would cause them no damage. (We would not remove a kidney from a temporarily comatose person, even if that individual would function as well as he is functioning with a single kidney.)

If, as we have argued, embryos are human beings, then it

seems straightforwardly wrong to subject them to experiments and procedures that would be rightly recognized by all as forms of assault if performed on human beings at later developmental stages. To think otherwise is to be guilty of a form of discrimination based upon age; not, to be sure, as great a form of discrimination as that practiced by those who destroy human embryos, but an unjust form of treatment nonetheless.

We judge then that adult stem cell research, dedifferentiation of somatic cells, and altered nuclear transfer are all worthy of investment and exploration and might provide ethically feasible ways of procuring pluripotent human stem cells. We are also interested in seeing if progress can be made in distinguishing organismically dead from living embryos in cryopreservation, though this is probably not a long-term solution. In any event, these possible strategies for devising non-embryo-destructive ways of obtaining pluripotent stem cells make it clear that science involving such cells needn't be brought to a halt by a decision to respect the lives of embryonic human beings. Nor should it: as we have argued, the state exists not just to defend but to promote the well-being of its citizens. If certain avenues of research offer the hope of significant medical progress without compromising the well-being of the youngest human beings among us, then the state ought to offer such encouragement as is necessary to bring such research to fruition. Accordingly, we offer the following proposal:

The Technological Proposal: The United States should significantly increase federal funding for research into adult, amniotic, and placental stem cells.

Moreover, scientists should pursue, and the state should support, research into the dedifferentiation of somatic cells, altered nuclear transfer, and techniques to distinguish dead from living cryopreserved embryos.

THE CULTURAL QUESTION

Finally, it is necessary to raise a combined moral and cultural question, a question that Ronald Green's essay pointed us toward. A large part of the impetus, it is clear, toward embryonic stem cell research comes from the fact that there are simply so many embryos condemned to perpetual cryopreservation or eventual incineration. It is certainly an unprecedented circumstance in human history—hundreds of thousands of nascent human beings in a kind of limbo with little hope of being brought to maturity. What is a reasonable response to this state of affairs for those who are convinced, as we are, of the humanity of the embryo? This question is too great for us to address to anyone's satisfaction. We wish only to indicate two of the ways in which we think it should be answered.

One necessary response is clear: the practice of creating and freezing extra embryos as part of IVF should give us serious moral pause. At the very least, this practice should come to an end if we wish to be a culture that treasures life and children, and not one that commodifies, instrumentalizes, and mechanizes them. Reform of the assisted reproduction industry should therefore rank high on a list of partial solutions to the moral and cultural question concerning excess human embryos. We might, to begin with, look to Italy's example in this area: under Italian law, it is impermissible for couples to fertilize more than three eggs, and all successfully created embryos must be implanted in the mother.

A second avenue that we believe should be given serious moral consideration is that of embryo adoption. In the past few years, this option has been pursued with greater frequency, often by families who wish to *rescue* frozen embryos from their inhuman fate. There are still those who question whether this can be done with moral propriety, and with some of their fears we agree. For example, if the primary motive for embryo adoption becomes a woman's desire to carry a child in her own womb, then we seem dangerously close to treating children as a means to satisfying our own desires. But if embryo adoption is done as a loving response on the part of a married couple to the needs of a very young child, then it seems potentially on a moral par with traditional adoption, and consistent with a respect for human life. Similarly, embryo rescue without adoption—i.e., the child is put up for adoption after birth—might be a form of service that women could perform on behalf of these youngest of human beings. Accordingly, we offer the following proposal to address the cultural question:

The Cultural Proposal: The United States should legally regulate the production of human embryos in IVF procedures to ensure that couples create no more embryos than they could reasonably expect to bring to term. To address the fate of the millions of embryos currently trapped in cryopreservation, adoption agencies should coordinate with assisted reproduction clinics and hospitals to offer the opportunity to couples to

adopt embryos whose biological parents are unable or unwilling to bring them to term.

Our final proposal might bring to mind the story with which we began our book, the story of Noah and the flood. Noah's story is so inspiring, we believe, because it is so clear that his rescuers saved a particular person's life—Noah's, in fact. Yet it cannot be denied that there are many more human persons in precisely the same predicament as was Noah, and whose need for rescue is independent of the contingencies of the weather. Our country needs to turn its attention to their fate, not by making use of them, as if they were mere biological material, but by acknowledging their fundamental humanity and the obligations we have to protect and promote their lives, from their beginnings to their natural ends.

Notes

CHAPTER 1

1. When, and even whether, embryonic stem cell research will prove to be therapeutically useful is a highly speculative matter, notwithstanding the grand claims that have been made on its behalf by those seeking to persuade the public to support it with taxpayer dollars.

2. For example, the Center for Genetics and Society supports embryonic stem cell research but has been critical of the lack of independent oversight that characterizes the operations of the California Institute for Regenerative Medicine, which is in charge of the multibillion-dollar research initiative: http://www.genetics-and-society .org/.

3. See G. Annas and M. Grodin, *The Nazi Doctors and the Nuremberg Code: Human Rights in Human Experimentation* (Oxford, England: Oxford University Press, 1992); James H. Jones, *Bad Blood: The Tuskegee Syphilis Experiment* (New York: The Free Press, 1993); Advisory Committee on Human Radiation Experiments, *The Human Radiation Experiments* (Oxford, England: Oxford University Press, 1996).

4. Was the embryo in the petri dish Louise Brown? Or did Louise come into existence sometime later? Here we should again recall our story of the embryonic Noah's rescue. We can also listen to Robert Edwards's own testimony: Thus, recollecting (at her birth) his appreciation

of Louise Brown as one or two cells in his petri dish, Edwards [said]: "She was beautiful then and she is beautiful now." Robert Edwards and Patrick Steptoe, *A Matter of Life* (London: Arrow 1981). Edwards and his coauthor accurately describe the embryo as "a microscopic human being—one in its very earliest stages of development" (p. 83). They say that the human being in the embryonic stage of development is "passing through a critical period in its life of great exploration: it becomes magnificently organized, switching on its own biochemistry, increasing in size, and preparing itself quickly for implantation in the womb" (p. 97).

5. Center for Applied Reproductive Science, "In Vitro Fertilization and Embryo Transfer," available at: http://www.ivf-et.com/tlc/fact_ivf.html#5.

6. Kenneth J. Ryan, "The Politics and Ethics of Human Embryo and Stem Cell Research," in Michael Ruse and Christopher Tynes, eds., *The Stem Cell Controversy* (Amherst, NY: Prometheus Books, 2003), p. 214. The EAB noted, however, that by "ethically acceptable" it did not mean "clearly ethical," but rather "ethically defensible but still legitimately controverted." 44 *Federal Register*, 35033–58 (June 18, 1997), p. 35055.

7. Richard Doerflinger, "The Policy and Politics of Embryonic Stem Cell Research," *The National Catholic Bioethics Quarterly* 1 (2001), pp. 135–43; see especially pp. 138–39.

8. See Ronald M. Green, *The Human Embryo Research Debates: Bioethics in the Vortex of Controversy* (New York: Oxford University Press, 2001).

9. Doerflinger, p. 139.

10. "Ethical Issues in Human Stem Cell Research," National Bioethics Advisory Commission, September 1999, p. 71. Available online at: http://www.georgetown.edu/research/nrcbl/nbac/stemcel.pdf.

11. Ibid., p. 72.

12. The claim that these cells ("embryonic stem cells") are pluripotent is based on their gross morphology and cell-typical surface markers. Additional research is necessary to establish the true functional identity or equivalence of these cells to their natural counterparts.

13. Maureen Condic, "The Basics about Stem Cells," *First Things* 119 (January 2002), pp. 30–31.

14. J. A. Thomson, J. Itskovitz-Eldor, S. S. Shapiro, et al., "Em-

bryonic Stem Cell Lines Derived from Human Blastocysts," *Science* 282 (1998), pp. 1145–47.

15. Condic, p. 32.

16. I. Wilmut et al., "Viable Offspring Derived from Fetal and Adult Mammalian Cells," *Nature* (February 27, 1997), pp. 810–13. We say "genetically *virtually* identical," because although the nucleus of the cell, which contains the chromosomes, carries more than 99 percent of the DNA, there is a tiny amount of DNA in the mitochondria (a part of the cell associated with energy production) that is retained within the cytoplasm of the enucleated egg. Only if the egg and the somatic cell nucleus come from the same female will the embryo be a genetically completely identical clone.

17. See Lee Silver, *Remaking Eden: Cloning and Beyond in a Brave New World* (New York: Avon Books, 1997).

18. Coaxing these cells to form later, producing more differentiated cell types for possible therapeutic use, is proving to be an extraordinary technological challenge. In natural embryogenesis, differentiation takes place within a complex cellular microenvironment. Cell-to-cell signals from adjacent cells within this niche take place in a complex spatiotemporal pattern. Replicating such a complex microenvironment has proven to be exceedingly difficult. The exaggerated promises made early in the debate have been revised, and many scientists now candidly admit that such therapies are at best decades away. Beyond this, cell therapies would involve hundreds of millions, perhaps billions of cells for the treatment of an individual patient. Assuring purity of cell culture will not be easy, given the tendency of these cells to develop chromosomal abnormalities. To date, there has been little progress overcoming the unfortunate tendency of these cells to form tumors (teratomas) when transplanted into experimental animal subjects.

19. This passage appears in an expert report submitted by Dr. Lee M. Silver to John Zen Jackson, Esq., of May 30, 2003, wherein Silver offers expert testimony in the case of *Acuna v. Turkish*, New Jersey (Appellate Docket # A-4022-03T5). Silver quotes this passage in his book, *Challenging Nature: The Clash of Science and Spirituality at the New Frontiers of Life* (New York: Harper Collins, 2006), pp. 116–18.

20. In addition, as will become clear in chapters three and six in

particular, the findings of science must be supplemented by philosophical arguments, particularly when the import of the scientific findings is called into question.

CHAPTER 2

1. T. W. Sadler, *Langman's Medical Embryology*, 9th ed. (Baltimore, MD: Lippincott, Williams, and Wilkins, 2004), p. 3.

2. William Larsen, *Human Embryology*, 3rd ed. (Philadelphia: Churchill Livingstone, 2001), p. 4.

3. We are speaking here of the normal case. Not infrequently, an embryo comes into existence with an abnormal complement of chromosomes. Although this generally causes the early death of the embryo, in some cases live birth and survival even into adulthood occurs, as, for example, sometimes in trisomy 21, commonly known as Down syndrome.

4. We are grateful to human embryologist Dr. Ward Kischer for pointing out that the X and Y chromosomes "are not completely homologous—but that there is a homologous region on both so that they actually pair end to end."

5. Campbell Reece, *Biology*, 7th ed. (New York: Pearson, 2005), p. 240.

6. Bruce Carlson's book is especially helpful regarding the role of hormones and enzymes: Bruce Carlson, *Human Embryology and Developmental Biology* (St. Louis: C. V. Mosby, 2004).

7. Keith L. Moore and T. V. N. Persaud, *The Developing Human*, 7th ed. (New York: W. B. Saunders, 2003), p. 34.

8. Larsen, p. 3.

9. Moore and Persaud, p. 16.

10. Nicanor Pier Giorgio Austriaco, O.P., "On Static Eggs and Dynamic Embryos: A Systems Perspective," *The National Catholic Bioethics Quarterly*, Winter 2002, pp. 666–67.

11. Moore and Persaud, p. 37.

12. Sadler, pp. 42–43. The term *embryo proper* has caused some unfortunate confusion. In the language of embryology, this term is not meant to designate what defines the embryo, but rather what parts of the embryo will provide the cell lineages that will form the cells and tissues of the postnatal human. Clearly, the component parts of the

embryo are just that, parts *of the embryo*. The supporting membranes (placenta, amnion, and chorion) and their progenitors are rightly considered intrauterine organs—essential parts of the whole organism.

13. Moore and Persaud, p. 37.

14. Carlson, p. 53.

15. In some, and perhaps many cases, what is lost is not an embryo but a nonembryonic entity resulting from defects in the fertilization process. Interestingly, some of these entities will form blastocysts, but this does not mean that they are actually embryos. It is an error to infer from the fact that all embryos go through a blastocyst stage that every entity forming a blastocyst is therefore an embryo.

16. Moore and Persaud, p. 44.

17. Ibid., p. 47.

18. Ibid., p. 16 (emphasis added).

19. Larsen, p. 1 (emphasis added).

20. Ronan O'Rahilly and Fabiola Müller, *Human Embryology and Teratology* (New York: Wiley-Liss, 2001), p. 8.

21. Carlson, p. 64.

22. Moore and Persaud, p. 67.

23. A complete hydatidiform mole is a diploid conceptus with only paternal chromosomes. It can form when an oocyte loses the female pronuclei and two sperm enter the egg, each contributing a haploid pronucleus that fuse to form a diploid nucleus, or when one sperm enters the oocyte and its haploid pronucleus reproduces to form a diploid nucleus. In either case, the result is a disordered growth, as it lacks maternal chromosomes. Partial hydatidiform moles are triploid; that is, they contain one set of maternal chromosomes with *two* sets of paternal chromosomes. These organisms do display signs of embryonic development and indications that they are defective embryos. Complete hydatidiform moles, however, do not. See Larsen, pp. 44–47, for further details. Teratomas are of disputed origin. They are a class of tumors that appear to arise from pluripotent germ cells. That is, they occur in females when an oocyte begins to develop without being fertilized. These growths can often contain adult tissues such as hair, teeth, and patches of skin, but they lack an organized structure of development and cohering principle. For more, see Larsen, p. 31.

CHAPTER 3

1. Plato, "Phaedo," in *The Republic and Other Works*, trans. B. Jowett (New York: Anchor Books, 1973), p. 498.

2. René Descartes, *Meditations on First Philosophy*, trans. Donald W. Cress (Indianapolis: Hackett Publishing Company, 1979), p. 49.

3. Saint Thomas Aquinas, *Commentary on Paul's First Letter to the Corinthians XV*, pp. 1, 11.

4. John Locke, *Essay Concerning Human Understanding*, ed. H. P. Nidditch (Oxford, England: Clarendon Press, 1979), Essay II, xxvii #9, p. 246.

5. Our discussion here is indebted to Alfonso Gomez-Lobo, "Sortals and Human Beginnings," available online at: http://ontology.buffalo.edu/medicine_and_metaphysics/Gomez-Lobo.doc.

6. J. McMahan, "Cloning, Killing, and Identity," *Journal of Medical Ethics* 25 (1999), p. 83.

7. Lynne Rudder Baker, *Persons and Bodies: A Constitution View* (Cambridge, England: Cambridge University Press, 2000).

8. For further reflections along these lines, and an excellent presentation of a unified view of the human person as both animal and spirit, see David Braine, *The Human Person: Animal and Spirit* (Notre Dame, IN: University of Notre Dame Press, 1992).

9. Indeed, some philosophers hold that the person is merely a series of events or experiences spread out in time. In this view, the person never exists as a whole entity, but only as a series of "time slices," the sum of which is the human person. It is not clear that this view is coherent: how can time slices with no temporal extension produce a temporally extended series?

10. Eric Olson, *The Human Animal: Identity Without Psychology* (Oxford, England: Oxford University Press, 1997).

11. John Finnis, Joseph M. Boyle, Jr., and Germain Grisez, *Nuclear Deterrence, Morality and Realism* (Oxford, England: Oxford University Press, 1987), pp. 308–9.

12. Baker, p. 124.

13. Ibid., p. 164 (our emphasis).

14. Ibid., p. 124, quoting Eric Olson, "Was I Ever a Fetus?" *Philosophy and Phenomenological Research* 57 (1997), p. 97.

CHAPTER 4

1. Jeremy Bentham, *An Introduction to the Principles of Morals and Legislation* (New York: Hafner Publishing Co., 1948), p. 2.

2. Ibid., p. 947.

3. Ibid., p. 950.

4. John Stuart Mill, *Utilitarianism* (Indianapolis, IN: Hackett Publishing Co., 1979), p. 8.

5. Ibid., p. 11.

6. Alasdair MacIntyre, *After Virtue*, 2nd ed. (Notre Dame, IN: University of Notre Dame Press, 1984), p. 64.

7. Peter Singer, *Practical Ethics* (Cambridge, England: Cambridge University Press, 1993), p. 57.

8. Immanuel Kant, *Groundwork of the Metaphysics of Morals*, trans. Mary Gregor (Cambridge, England: Cambridge University Press, 1998), p. 31.

9. Ibid., p. 38.

10. Alan Donagan, *The Theory of Morality* (Chicago: University of Chicago Press, 1977), p. 83.

11. Our understanding of natural law theory is indebted especially to Germain Grisez, Joseph Boyle, and John Finnis. See Germain Grisez, "The First Principle of Practical Reason: A Commentary on the Summa Theologiae, 1–2 Question 94, Article 2," *Natural Law Forum* 10 (1965), pp. 168–201; Germain Grisez, Joseph Boyle, and John Finnis, "Practical Principles, Moral Truth, and Ultimate Ends," *American Journal of Jurisprudence* 32 (1987), pp. 99–151; and John Finnis, *Natural Law and Natural Rights* (Oxford, England: The Clarendon Press, 1980).

12. Charity demands that we believe this of most who engage in destructive research on human embryos. Yet the facts on occasion, at least, diverge from such an interpretation. Consider the case of the South Korean scientist Hwang Woo-suk, whose work on human cloning has recently been revealed to be almost entirely fraudulent. Such scandals speak to the possibility of radical failures in the ethics of science; could scientists be inclined to such failures in a special way when they are engaged in research that is for other reasons immoral, such as research that involves the destruction of embryonic human life?

13. We do not here address the troubled question of killing for

retributive purposes, as in the capital punishment of those who have been justly convicted of heinous murders. People associated with the ethical theory we have set forth here have argued on different sides of this question, as have Kantians and utilitarians.

14. As Princeton professor Jeffrey Stout observed in a conference at which he spoke, in response to a question about how he could believe in human dignity and human rights while at the same time professing atheism, one need not believe in God in order to appreciate the moral significance of the human possession of powers traditionally ascribed to divinity. Thus, even an unbeliever like Professor Stout could join us in affirming that human dignity is rooted in godlike attributes.

CHAPTER 5

1. David Boonin, *A Defense of Abortion* (Cambridge, England: Cambridge University Press, 2003), pp. xiii–xiv.

2. Material from this section is drawn from an essay by Robert P. George and Patrick Lee, "The Wrong of Abortion," in Andrew I. Cohen and Christopher Wellman, eds., *Contemporary Debates in Applied Ethics* (New York: Blackwell Publishers, 2005), pp. 13–26.

3. Judith Jarvis Thomson, "Abortion," *Boston Review*, 1995, available online at http://www.bostonreview.net/BR20.3/thomson.html.

4. Both Peter Singer and Michael Tooley have accepted this implication: see Peter Singer, *Practical Ethics*, 2nd ed. (Cambridge, England: Cambridge University Press, 1993); Michael Tooley, *Abortion and Infanticide* (New York: Oxford University Press, 1983).

5. Michael Sandel, *The Case Against Perfection: Ethics in the Age of Genetic Engineering* (Cambridge, MA: Harvard University Press, 2007), p. 118.

6. Ibid., pp. 118–19.

7. Ronald Green, *The Human Embryo Research Debates: Bioethics in the Vortex of Controversy* (Oxford, England: Oxford University Press, 2001), p. 32.

8. Ibid.

9. Ibid., p. 49.

10. Ibid., p. 39.

11. Carson Strong, "The Moral Status of Preembryos, Embryos,

Fetuses and Infants," *The Journal of Medicine and Philosophy* 22 (1997), 457–78; quotation p. 467.

12. Ibid., p. 468.

13. Ibid., p. 470.

14. Bruce Carlson, *Human Embryology and Developmental Embryology* (St. Louis: C. V. Mosby, 2004), p. 58; Keith L. Moore and T. V. N. Persaud, *The Developing Human*, 7th ed. (New York: W. B. Saunders, 2003), p. 40.

15. This is clearly the case in trisomy 21, commonly called Down syndrome. Trisomy cases involve the presence of extra genetic material in a particular chromosomal pair; in many cases of Down syndrome, there is an extra chromosome in the twenty-first pair. Even though the extra chromosome might be considered a defect in the program itself, a Down syndrome child nevertheless has, as a complete hydatidiform mole does not, the developmental program of a human being. The same is true of anencephalic infants, who do not develop a complete brain. What would have to be known in any particular case of chromosomal abnormality was whether the defect was such as to eliminate entirely the active capacity for self-directed growth to a point where the human capacities for thought and choice could not be actualized. Only in such cases would there be no human being at all.

16. Professor Sandel asked this question of Robert George. The question is posed, with slightly different details, in Sandel, p. 122, who attributes it to George J. Annas, "A French Homunculus in a Tennessee Court," *Hastings Center Report* 19 (1989), pp. 20–22.

CHAPTER 6

1. See John Locke, *An Essay Concerning Human Understanding* (Amherst, NY: Prometheus Books, 1995), part II, ch xxvii; see also Peter van Inwagen's discussion in *Material Beings* (Ithaca, NY: Cornell University Press, 1990), chapter fourteen, 142–68.

2. Van Inwagen, pp. 153–54.

3. Barry Smith and Berit Brogaard, "Sixteen Days," *The Journal of Medicine and Philosophy* 28 (2003), p. 55.

4. Keith L. Moore and T. V. N. Persaud, *The Developing Human*, 7th ed. (New York: W. B. Saunders, 2003), p. 44.

5. Ronan O'Rahilly and Fabiola Müller, *Human Embryology and Teratology* (New York: Wiley-Liss, 2001), p. 74; Moore and Persaud, p. 37; William Larsen, *Human Embryology*, 3rd ed. (Philadelphia: Churchill Livingstone, 2001), pp. 18–21.

6. Moore and Persaud, p. 37.

7. Smith and Brogaard, pp. 55–56.

8. Bruce Carlson, *Human Embryology and Developmental Biology* (St. Louis: C. V. Mosby, 2004), p. 41.

9. Patrick Lee, "A Christian Philosopher's View of Recent Directions in the Abortion Debate," *Christian Bioethics* 10, vol. 10 (2004), p. 12; Lee cites a number of studies. We should note, however, that scientists continue to discuss the validity of these findings; see Gretchen Vogel, "Embryologists Polarized over Early Cell Fate Determination," *Science*, vol. 308, May 6, 2005.

10. Carlson, p. 44.

11. Ibid., p. 45.

12. Also see: Philip G. Peters Jr., "The Ambiguous Meaning of Human Conception," *UC Davis Law Review* 40 (2006), pp. 199ff.

13. For a thorough and balanced summary of recent research: Magdalena Zernicka-Goetz, "The First Cell-Fate Decisions in the Mouse Embryo: Destiny Is a Matter of Both Chance and Choice," *Current Opinion in Genetics and Development* 16 (2006), pp. 406–12, online at http//www.sciencedirect.com. Also see, for example, James W. Zimmerman and Richard M. Shultz, "Analysis of Gene Expression in the Preimplantation Mouse Embryo: Use of mRNA Differential Display," *Proceedings of the National Academy of Science USA, Developmental Biology* 91 (1994), pp. 5456–60; Jo-Ann L. Stanton, Andrew B. Macgregor, and David P. L. Green, "Gene Expression in the Mouse Preimplantation Embryo," *Reproduction* 125 (2003), pp. 457–68.

14. The possibility of twinning, of splitting into two individuals, provides no evidence at all against the present existence of an individual prior to the splitting taking place. From the fact that *A* can split into *B* and *C*, it simply does not follow, nor does the fact at all suggest, that *A* was not an individual before the division. Logically speaking, there are three possibilities. *A* might have been an amalgam or aggregate of *A* and *B*. But also *A* might have ceased to exist and *B* and *C* have come to be

from the constituents that once went into *A* (though we do not think this is the most plausible account of what happens in human monozygotic twinning). Or, finally, it is possible that *A* was an individual and is identical with *B* or *C*; that is, that a new individual is generated by the splitting off from the whole of which it once was a part (which we think is the most likely account of what goes on in most cases of human monozygotic twinning). So the mere fact of the division does nothing to show that, prior to the division, *A* could not have been a determinate, single individual (though itself composed of parts).

It is possible that with monozygotic twinning the original organism dies and gives rise to two new organisms—contrary to what Evan Graboyes suggests, we see nothing absurd in that situation. However, we think that this is not what occurs, at least in most cases, since in many instances there is an obvious unity of plan of development between the zygote, on the one hand, and one (but not both) of the twins, on the other hand. An example occurs with some twins in whom only one suffers from trisomy 21: evidently, one of the twins is generated by the splitting and exhibits a unique plan of development that differs from the other twin. See: J. G. Rogers, S. M. Voullaire, and H. Gold, "Monozygotic Twins Discordant for Trisomy 21," *American Journal of Human Genetics* 11 (1982), pp. 143–46; T. Hassold, "Mosaic Trisomies in Human Spontaneous Abortions," *Human Genetics* 11 (1982), pp. 31–35; Angelo Serra and Roberto Columbo, "The Identity and Status of the Human Embryo: The Contribution of Biology," in Juan de Dios Vial Correa and Elio Sgreccia's *The Identity and Status of the Human Embryo, Proceedings of the Third Assembly of the Pontifical Academy for Life* 169 (Vaticana: Lebreria Editrice, 1999).

Monozygotic twinning is, of course, comparatively rare. Most monozygotic twinning (between 65 and 90 percent) occur between the fifth and ninth days after fertilization, and the twins share a common chorion but each has his own amnion. Only between 10 percent and 33 percent of the cases of monozygotic twinning occur before the fifth day so that each twin has both his own amnion and his own chorion. (See Keith Moore and T. V. N. Persuad, *The Developing Human*, 7th ed. [New York: W. B. Saunders, 2003], p. 147; Carlson, p. 55.) Perhaps some cases of twinning occur in the first cleavage, where a one-celled embryo (a zygote) divides into two one-celled embryos. It is more likely in this type of case than in others that the first human embryo ceases to exist and gives rise to two others.

15. Ronald Bailey, "Are Stem Cells Babies?" *Reasononline*, July 11, 2001, online at: http://reason.com/rb/rb071101.shtml.

16. Ibid.

17. Lee Silver, "The Biotech Culture Clash: Embedded Religious Perspectives in East and West Create Distinct Responses to Genetic Engineering," July 18, 2006, online at http://www.checkbiotech.org/root/index.cfm?fuseaction=subtopics&topic_id=5&subtopic_id=20&doc_id=13159&start=1&control=227&page_start=1&page_nr=151&pg=1.

18. Letter of Lee Silver to John Zen Jackson, Ésq., of May 30, 2003, wherein Silver offers expert testimony in the case of *Acuna v. Turkish*, New Jersey (Appellate Docket # A-4022–03T5), p. 6.

19. Ibid., p. 5.

20. Ibid., p. 6.

21. Ibid.

22. Strictly speaking, embryos are neither fertilized nor unfertilized. Fertilization of the oocyte, when complete, generates an embryo.

23. Silver, p. 7.

CHAPTER 7

1. Material from this section is drawn from Patrick Lee and Robert P. George, "Acorns and Embryos," *The New Atlantis* 7 (Fall 2004/Winter 2005), pp. 90–100.

2. Michael J. Sandel, "Embryo Ethics—The Moral Logic of Stem Cell Research," *New England Journal of Medicine* 351 (July 15, 2004), pp. 207–9: quotation is from p. 208.

3. Michael J. Sandel, "Dr. Sandel Replies" (letter to the editor), *The New England Journal of Medicine* 351 (October 14, 2004), pp. 1689–90.

4. Paul R. McHugh, M.D., "Zygote and 'Clonote'—the Ethical Use of Embryonic Stem Cells," *The New England Journal of Medicine* 351 (July 15, 2004), pp. 209–11; quotation on p. 210.

5. Ibid.

6. Ibid.

7. Gene Outka, "The Ethics of Human Stem Cell Research," *Kennedy Institute of Ethics Journal* 12 (2002), pp. 175–213; quote p. 193.

8. Ibid.

9. Ibid., p. 194.

10. Ibid., p. 202.

11. Ibid., p. 204.

12. Ibid., p. 203.

13. Ibid., p. 205.

14. Ronald M. Green, "Benefiting from 'Evil': An Incipient Moral Problem in Human Stem Cell Research," *Bioethics* 16 (2002), pp. 544–56; quote p. 553.

15. Ibid.

16. Ibid., p. 554.

17. Ibid.

18. Ibid., p. 555.

19. Ibid.

20. Ibid.

CHAPTER 8

1. See John Rawls, *Political Liberalism* (New York: Columbia University Press, 1993).

2. See Judith Jarvis Thomson, "Abortion," *Boston Review* 1995; available online at http://www.bostonreview.net/BR20.3/thomson.html.

3. The President's Council on Bioethics, "Alternative Sources of Human Pluripotent Stem Cells," May 2005; available online at www.bioethics.gov.

4. See William B. Hurlbut, "Altered Nuclear Transfer as a Morally Acceptable Means for the Procurement of Human Embryonic Stem Cells," *Perspectives in Biology and Medicine* 48 (2005), pp. 211–29.

5. "Alternative Sources of Human Pluripotent Stem Cells," p. 37.

6. For a defense of the claim that the entity created in ANT is not a human embryo, see E. Christian Brugger, "Moral Stem Cells," *First Things* 163 (May 2006), pp. 15–17.

Index